Mean Drunk

Anger, Hostility and Alcohol

William Tappan

Mean Drunk
Anger, Hostility and Alcohol

William Tappan

ISBN-10: 1493556673
ISBN-13: 978-1493556670

CreateSpace Independent Publishing Platform
Charleston, SC

Edited by Molly and Jim Cameron of Cameron Editorial
Services, mj.edit@cox.net

Cover design by Steve Levine

Thanks to Alli Von Mohr for her help on the print
edition cover.

Thanks to my friends who generously shared their
personal experiences and brought life to this mysterious
puzzle.

William Tappan has been a member of the Authors
Guild since 1979. This is his seventh book.

Email: meandrunkbook@gmail.com

Contents

Foreword

This book has much to offer to a number of different populations, including individuals who are heavy drinkers of alcohol, family members and others in close proximity to the heavy drinkers, psychologists and psychiatrists, other health care providers, police and other protectors of public safety, and alcohol researchers. Specifically, this book provides a clear understanding of the causes, contexts, and consequences of violent behavior associated with heavy drinking of alcohol.

Episodes of violent behavior, including domestic fights, bar-room brawls, and other situations, are frequently reported in the popular press. Very often it is mentioned that drinking of alcohol is involved. However, while heavy use of alcohol is considered to increase the risk of violence, rarely has the cause of the violence been directly attributed to the alcohol.

There are probably a number of reasons why alcohol is not identified by many as the direct cause of the aggressive behavior. Perhaps one of the reasons that alcohol is not considered to be the cause of the behavior is that no specific underlying mechanism has been described that could explain the role of alcohol in causing the aggression.

What is very significant in this book, *Mean Drunk*, is that William Tappan presents a plausible hypothesis to explain how drinking alcohol is directly responsible for the aggression. The underlying neural mechanisms involve specific effects, including neurochemistry, of the alcohol on the brains of susceptible individuals directly causing the aggression.

He defines the problem as the hostility reaction to alcohol, or HRA, which is the neurological response of the brain to the alcohol. HRA includes the full spectrum of aggressive behaviors caused by the alcohol. The greater the amount of alcohol taken in and the faster it is consumed, the more the occurrence of HRA and the greater the occurrence of blackouts.

Blackouts are a very common complication of heavy drinking, even among social drinkers. Blackouts result in the individual having no memory of the events which occurred during the drinking. Thus, individuals having HRA frequently have no awareness of what took place when they were drinking, and, therefore, take no responsibility for their aggressive behavior.

By increasing awareness and understanding of HRA, this book provides an opportunity for persons with heavy drinking to change their pattern of behavior and for persons who are the target of HRA to understand that they are not the cause of the problem.

Stan Handmaker, M.D., Ph.D.,
Professor Emeritus of Pediatrics and Psychiatry
University of New Mexico School of Medicine

Preface

This book is about the hostility that flows from drinking alcohol: moods that become mean, words that become weapons, and confrontations that become physical. Hostile aggression is the central outcome of drinking for those who are susceptible, and a major defining characteristic of intoxication. Hostility and alcohol are linked relatives, but little has been written that clarifies their relationship. What follows is about the connection between hostility and alcohol and the underlying neurobiology.

The purpose of *Mean Drunk* is to contribute to the understanding of this major problem. In the process, I hope to help individuals who are caught in the web of chaos characteristic of heavy-drinking hostility. The first step is to define the problem. To do this, I introduce the hostility reaction to alcohol—HRA. This new concept is a start for sorting out the anger and hostility that so many people are susceptible to.

Next, I frame the cause, context, and consequence of the anger and hostility. The cause is a constant in all contexts, the result of a neurobiological reaction to alcohol in the areas of the brain associated with aggression. The context is the setting of HRA, which often is mischaracterized as a cause, such as domestic violence, air rage, and bar fights. The consequences from each context are ruined relationships, prison terms, and worse.

Mean Drunk is the product of a lifelong effort to solve a puzzle, which started in my childhood. I grew up in a heavy-drinking household and followed the tradition into college and beyond until age 40, when I realized that I had to choose between alcohol and the person I wanted to be. What followed was 25 years of research that is distilled in *Mean Drunk*.

With understanding come awareness and freedom to choose: The end result is self-reliance and a more productive and happy life. If you are personally affected by the hostility flowing from drinking alcohol, I hope *Mean Drunk* will help you — if that's the path you choose.

Chapter One

From Drinking to Aggression

"The Beer Made Us Do It"

At summer's end, four friends walked along a river bank. Six packs in each hand held the promise of a night of more fun, after spending a day drinking in a local bar. They settled in the protection of the cottonwoods and began some serious drinking, laughing and loud talking. No one bothered them along this stretch of the river. It was all theirs.

The details of what happened next are fuzzy. The end result is not. About six hours into this extended holiday get-together, hostilities interrupted the planned fun. Three got mad at one. With heavy rocks, they crushed the target's head, leaving him dead under the cottonwoods.

It probably began with a word—it usually does. Maybe there was a hostile comment or perceived insult that turned the laughter ugly. Words became the trigger for physical confrontation, followed by attack and murder.

The cause was not the argument. The words exchanged are now long forgotten, if they were ever remembered. At trial no rational justification was offered. It was much more direct, as explained by one of the suffering-surviving three: "The beer made us do it." They probably know what they are talking about, given the first-hand nature of their experience. We should listen to them. [1]

Sometimes you just have to pay attention to what happens in real life. There are four suffering victims in this story. One's suffering was short. Three must live with what they did.

And Then What Happens?

What is it in some people that turns fun with drinking into hostile confrontation? Is it a side effect — a reaction to the alcohol? Or is it a hostility reaction to drinking alcohol — a hostility reaction to alcohol. We could shorten it to HRA.

The hostility reaction to alcohol (HRA) is a spectrum of aggressive behaviors that involves verbal and physical fighting, with several degrees of severity between the two. The outcome is often a ruined relationship, and sometimes death. How many of us have had the holiday experience of alcohol-fueled hostility among family members? You get together for some holiday cheer and sit down for dinner — and then what happens?

Do you dread the holidays? If you do, you probably know what happens next. Typically, one or two members of the family become hostile toward each other or a selected target — maybe a repeat target, selected because that person can't or won't fight back. Awkward times, these cheerful-hostile holidays, whether you are a target or an observer.

First the drinking, then the mood change, followed by words used as weapons, directed with the skill of a practiced fighter. Maybe physical conflict is on the holiday menu— a slap in the face of a husband or wife gone too far across the HRA spectrum, out of control, with total disregard for the civility expected during the holiday season. Suffering extends to everyone, with no lack of victims. All are puzzled and disappointed. Not exactly the festivity that was planned, but a predictable pattern when you understand the real cause.

If it's a predictable pattern, why the puzzle every time the hostility reaction surfaces? We humans have such a long history of alcohol-fueled arguments and physical violence that you might think there would be more public acknowledgement of the causal relationship. Has HRA become so common that we have cloaked the cause in a shroud of complacency? Part of the acknowledgement problem is that we don't have a simple name to describe what's going on. That's why HRA is useful. It's a handle that we can use to grasp the full spectrum of hostile, alcohol-caused behaviors— from personal belittling and constant criticism to physical assault and worse.

The Strange Case of Dr. Jekyll and Mr. Hyde

Robert Louis Stevenson, author of *The Strange Case of Dr. Jekyll and Mr. Hyde*, came as close as any to capturing the shape-shifting transformation characteristic of HRA. In the story, Dr. Jekyll attempts to develop a potion to enhance the pleasures of life by separating his good personality from his evil one, only to find that the evil Mr. Hyde takes him over completely. Both characters become victims— and both suffer. [2]

It's a strange case, this Jekyll and Hyde Syndrome. If you've seen the face of alcoholic sadism, you've seen Hyde, and, in the extreme, pure evil. He seems to have awakened from deep within the primitive areas of the brain, surfacing as control by his higher reasoning functions are compromised by alcohol. That's part of it, but there's more to this complex story.

The Jekyll and Hyde Syndrome describes certain behavior in The Big Book Alcoholics Anonymous uses in trying to understand the suffering an alcoholic can sometimes cause and experience:

"Here is the fellow that has been puzzling you, especially in his lack of control. He does absurd, incredible, tragic things while drinking. He is a real Dr. Jekyll and Mr. Hyde. He may be one of the finest fellows in the world. Yet let him drink for a day, and he frequently becomes disgustingly, and even dangerously anti-social." [3]

The difficulty in isolating a direct cause of the hostility reaction to alcohol is that some people don't have this reaction when they drink. I think Johnny Carson said it best in a 1979 *60 Minutes* interview with Mike Wallace: "Unlike many people who are happy and fun loving, I am the opposite. And it would happen just like that" (clapping his hands). He was describing his hostility reaction to alcohol. Mike Wallace added: "Take a drink and you wanted to take on the entire Russian army."[4]

Some people don't react with hostility. He did, and it was immediate. Carson's description fits a category in the manual used by psychiatrists to diagnose an unusual reaction to alcohol, called idiosyncratic intoxication:

"*Diagnostic criteria for Alcohol Idiosyncratic Intoxication*: A. Marked behavioral change, e.g., aggressive or assaultive behavior that is due to the recent ingestion of an amount of alcohol insufficient to induce intoxication in most people. B. The behavior is atypical of the person when not drinking. C. Not due to any other physical or mental disorder." [5]

What a straightforward description of HRA – clearly a consequence of drinking. Idiosyncratic intoxication highlights the impact of alcohol on the brain called HRA. We can't see exactly what is happening in the brain but we can see the hostility that results. Studying the neurobiology of people prone to idiosyncratic intoxication could be the gateway to learning more about the specific brain activity involved in the hostility reaction.

This 1980 third edition of the diagnostic manual – DSM III – also describes the more common diagnosis of alcohol intoxication: "A. Recent ingestion of alcohol (with no evidence suggesting that the amount was insufficient to cause intoxication in most people). B. Maladaptive behavioral effects, e.g., fighting, impaired judgment, interference with social or occupational functioning." The diagnostic criteria continue, describing the common physiological and the psychological signs of mood change and irritability. [6]

In 1987, a revised third edition replaced "fighting" with "disinhibition of sexual or aggressive impulses." [7] In 1994, the fourth edition changed the description to "inappropriate sexual or aggressive behavior," dropping the implication of cause contained in the word "disinhibition." [8]

The fifth edition – DSM V – was released in 2013. For our purposes, the diagnostic criteria of intoxication remained the same: "Clinically significant problematic behavioral or psychological changes (e.g., inappropriate sexual or aggressive behavior, mood lability, impaired judgment) that developed during, or shortly after, alcohol ingestion." [DSM V, p. 497]

DSM V also describes the general problem with alcohol abuse: "Alcohol use disorder is associated with a significant increase in the risk of accidents, violence, and suicide." It goes on to explain: "Severe problematic alcohol use also contributes to disinhibition and feelings of sadness and irritability, which contribute to suicide attempts and completed suicides." [DSM V, p. 496]

These are all good-faith attempts to describe a difficult phenomenon. The message remains the same with the newer, more inclusive description: a primary consequence of drinking can be aggression—and the acknowledgement of "inappropriate sexual" behavior certainly fits observed reality.

But "fighting" is concrete and expresses a solid physical or verbal expression of emotion. In contrast, "inappropriate sexual or aggressive behavior" is subjective and hangs in the air as an abstraction. Who decides what is "inappropriate"? There is little doubt about what a fight is. However, it's important that the aggressive and sexual components of intoxication have been acknowledged by the psychiatric community—and aggressive behavior certainly encompasses fighting. This is not the type of aggression you see in competitive sports or business. This is hostile aggression driven by the urge to hurt another person with words and/or physically.

With these distinctions in mind, our interest remains HRA in its both subtle and obvious expressions, and how it affects real people in real life. The HRA spectrum touches us all and costs us all.

Worse yet is what happens when a child witness is selected as the target. This is how demeaning words from parents become chisels, cutting a child's unformed self-image into a distorted shape of confusion that can take years to overcome—if ever.

There is often a sequence to this hostility spectrum. It starts with a mood change and irritability—then anger directed toward a convenient target, followed by a verbal attack laced with blame, and then perhaps a physical fight. In some situations, both the initial attacker and the target are intoxicated. Often the tables turn and the initial target becomes the attacker, fighting back, which makes for a muddled, if not impossible, confrontation incapable of being explained rationally.

To complicate things further, memory fails. Partial and complete blackouts by the drinker are common— perhaps even more common than usually recognized. [9] Expect hostility and blackouts from the drinker. Insert those two outcomes into your framework for understanding drinking and you will be on the road to making sense of the chaos.

Knowing Why Can Set You Free

Seeing the sadistic smile of Mr. Hyde emerge from a parent is proof positive of trouble ahead. This is no less so when a husband or wife sees the mood change and the emerging irritability that precedes an eruption of hostility from a spouse. It's common for a child to accept blame for the daily ritual of criticism, or a wife or husband to ask what they did wrong to cause such wrath. In both cases, there is an answer: you did nothing to precipitate the attack. You are simply in the path of a cascading hostility reaction to alcohol.

If you are trying to figure what you did wrong or what is wrong with you, understand that you didn't cause this alcohol reaction. HRA rests with the alcohol and the way it affects the drinker—not anything you did or are.

Ask yourself if the nightly, weekend, or holiday attacks would have occurred without the drinking, then understand that this aggression is caused by alcohol. [10] Where can you possibly be in this causal chain? You just had the bad luck to be a convenient target. You are not to blame. It's not your fault.

If you are drinking and attacking the friends, children, and spouse you love, think about it: did the beer make you do it, too? Awareness brings total responsibility in this case. Knowing about HRA brings full responsibility each and every time you choose to drink. The responsibility for drinking is yours and the consequences are on you. There are no excuses to be found in this book for your choice to drink or the behavior that follows.

It's strange how awareness brings the burden of responsibility—but it does. When you figure out something, it's time to take action and to get help if you need it. I once got into a conversation with a hard-working gardener who traveled from Mexico in the spring to earn money to support his family. Every so often he would ask a question, trying to figure out what made me tick.

Eventually, he asked me if I drank and I told him no, not for many years. He said he used to drink but stopped because it caused fights with his wife, who also drank. "When we drink we get into bad fights—real bad." He has a happy marriage now, and he and his wife have mutual control over how they treat each other. They are no longer subject to the effects of alcohol. Together, he and his wife recognized the obvious. This awareness resulted in taking responsibility for their choice to drink and marital happiness.

"I Didn't Do That"

Two friends were at a party. They were young, about 17 years old, and experienced drinkers for their age. It was a relatively small community, and weekend parties were a big part of the sparse social life. It was crowded in the living room where they sat on the couch. One got up to go to the bathroom and asked his friend to save the seat.

Within a minute a larger fellow walked up and sat down. The friend in charge of seat preservation informed the fellow that he couldn't sit there.

"Why not?"

"I'm saving it for my friend."

"Tough. I'm sitting here now."

Eventually, the friend returned and asked for his seat. The answer was again: "I'm sitting here now." This was too much for the seat protector:

"Really? Get the hell off this couch."

"Oh. You want to take this outside?"

"Sure, let's go."

The combatant who is more vicious usually determines the winner of a street fight, bar brawl or party confrontation. This one was no different. The seat thief never had a chance. Others eventually had to pull the seat-protecting friend off the poor fellow. As he told me: "I remember standing up to go outside. The next thing I remember was a crowd standing around me saying things like 'I didn't know you were a brawler, you destroyed that dude'. I looked back at him and said 'I didn't do that'."

"His face looked like Rocky Balboa at the end of the fight. I saw him again the next day; his face was all swollen. I have no memory of beating him. I still feel bad about it. I am not like that—not a fighter."

Blackouts, failed memory, and denial all run together in stories of heavy drinking. Mr. Hyde emerged to take over the persona of this young non-fighter, and his Dr. Jekyll half never remembered the visit. This is a stark episode in the life of someone who many years later still feels bad about what he did. He remembers not remembering and he remembers the crowd surrounding him in awe of his fighting ability—but that's all.

Even with no memory, he accepted the reality of what happened. Without witnesses, denial might describe his memory failure but, in this case, a complete blackout is what actually happened, as is often the case.

One of the strange things about alcohol is that it prevents formation of new long-term memories—the more and faster the drinking, the worse the memory loss. As the confrontation builds and the argument expands to verbal and physical attack, darkness deepens and memory fades. Blackouts can be partial or complete. [9]

I have seen the most condemning and belittling verbal attacks continue for what seems an interminable period, only to be followed by smiles and life-as-usual the next day. Really, there are two people in there. *The Strange Case of Dr. Jekyll and Mr. Hyde* is the norm in a heavy drinking home. Somehow alcohol closes the reflective function of the brain during and after confrontation, and normal consciousness withdraws to some unknown place—lost from the present.

Arguments between family members bring what seems to be denial the day after; but it may be as simple as a blackout—a failure to form new long-term memories while drunk. This strange and sometimes subtle side effect is not restricted to brawls. Simple conversations may never make it to memory. What the sober see as denial may, in some cases, be far more serious for the heavy drinker—lost memory and a transformed consciousness, creating a dark new persona in the eyes of the sober.

I often have wondered if a recorder or camera mounted strategically would come in handy the day after a drawn-out criticism fest. It seems harsh, but probably less so than attacks ignored, denied, or blacked out the next day. But to what end? Awareness of Mr. Hyde's visit forced on the Dr. Jekyll personality the next morning? Evidence of hostility preserved for the family history? Would it change anything or just trigger another fight?

Solutions are elusive. Awareness is always best when arrived at without force. So if you are entangled in this complicated hostility drama, consider developing a new perspective. Observe your role. Are you attacker or target, or at times both? Is this how you want to conduct your life? Do you have choices? What are they? It's really up to you to figure out.

No matter how you may fit into this scenario, you are the victim of an alcohol reaction that is often predictable, well-studied, and yet still a puzzle. Denial commonly is associated with refusal to acknowledge a drinking problem and centered on the inability to stop at will, but it gains real meaning when you are the target of HRA. This is the source of the puzzle. "How can she claim that she doesn't have a problem? Doesn't she remember what happened last night—the things she said?" Human puzzles often have missing pieces, and we tend to look for them in the wrong places, using reason when they are hiding in plain sight in some emotional and rationally inaccessible area of personality.

Reason is not involved in lost consciousness. The ability to reason is blacked out. Blackouts and denial are bookends for alcoholic consciousness, with several gradations between the two extremes, all reflecting degrees of lost consciousness and self-awareness. Maybe this loss is intentional. Maybe it is unconscious. Maybe it is a little of both.

Consider that alcohol can impair the reasoning ability of the prefrontal cortex and facilitate emotions from the limbic system. At the same time, it interacts with variations in genes that affect neurotransmission and express the personal history of the drinker. [11] Remember also that while alcohol is stirring up trouble, it can prevent memory formation of the events that follow—and who knows what else we haven't figured out so far. What a nasty combination of mental gymnastics that is.

"Tell Them I Don't Drink That Much"

My wife and I were talking with friends during dinner about someone they had known many years ago in Atlanta who had a serious drinking problem, with all the attack behaviors you can imagine. In this case, a drunk wife directed her criticism toward a compliant husband and various friends who visited from time to time. Our friends attempted to intervene. What happened next is a clear illustration of denial, blackouts, and meanness.

"We talked about her drinking throughout the whole two hours. It became surreal because she continued to insist that she didn't 'have a drinking problem'. She would say, 'Honey, tell them I don't drink that much.' And he would agree. When we reminded her of the mean things she just said to both of us, she would say she didn't say those things, and her husband would say he forgot what she said. So after two long hours — the first hour was spent telling us how mean we were to her — we just ended it because when someone is in that much denial and refuses to acknowledge any behavior, you can't discuss anything."

This is a good example of a repeat pattern you may recognize from your own experience. It's a personality modified by alcohol. Alcohol takes the unique-individual personality and replaces it with cookie-cutter behaviors that any experienced target would recognize as alcohol in control. An individual becomes a stereotypical drunk. What a life choice.

Did this drunk wife really forget the mean things she said to her friends? Or was she crafty in her reasoning and putting up a consistent stone wall of denial? Denial may not be intentional. It's more like a self-lie, to protect against self-awareness and the pain of the truth. Creating your own view of events and advocating it is typical of drunken behavior. Self-awareness is the first victim. The respect from others is the second.

In this case, shortly after the attempted intervention, a mutual friend attended a dinner party where the same woman was really drunk and talking about how bad drinking is: as if she had everybody fooled and was advocating an alterative reality with complete lack of reflection and self-awareness, trying to demonstrate to them that she was not drunk while being drunk. She was saying what she thought they wanted to hear, pandering to them so they would change their impression of her and spread the word of her new insight, confirming that she was not a problem-drinker. It was almost as if she was playing a childhood game of make-believe that everybody around her seemed to go along with. The only person she was fooling was herself, as she slowly chipped away at what remaining respect her friends may have had for her.

Lack of self-awareness, while still functioning physically and verbally, is common with practiced drinkers. Conscious denial when a drinker knows the words she speaks are not true is one thing. The unformed memory of a beating delivered at a party is at the opposite extreme. There are many degrees of self-awareness, or lack of awareness, between the two extremes.

We humans have the ability to complicate anything to the point of confusion. There are many variables, and consequently, opportunities to complicate things, when consciousness is involved. But if we understand what is happening, we can simplify and apply a little common sense and self-awareness to develop a useful framework.

HRA is a side effect of drinking—an alcohol reaction. Some drinkers don't experience it. Some react immediately with hostility and others only after prolonged bouts of drinking, or binge drinking.

Children and spouses living in a home with a heavy drinker who is moving back and forth between the Jekyll and Hyde personalities tend to focus on what they might have done to cause the criticism and ongoing abuse. In fact, they are not responsible for the behavior of the mean drunk. They are targets of a very nasty alcohol reaction that produces hostility.

One of the most puzzling aspects of HRA is the failure to remember the attack. There is often no feedback loop for the mean drunk that allows reflection on the hostility. Consequently, during the attack and after, there is a total lack of compassion for the target by the drinker—a mean and cruel thing to experience. It seems as if the personality shift from Jekyll to Hyde and back to Jekyll the day after is an expression of two different personalities, walled off from each other in a sick trick of consciousness called a blackout.

The message of HRA for the drinker is: know that you are the subject of an alcohol reaction; now that you know, the responsibility for drinking and the consequences are squarely on you. Understanding—and the awareness that follows—result in an unavoidable responsibility for your choice to drink. If you can't control your drinking, get help. That is the responsible thing to do. You are free to choose.

The message of HRA for the abused is: know you are on the receiving end of hostility that flows directly from the changes that alcohol causes in the brain. You are the target of a hostility reaction to alcohol. You are not to blame for the accusations contained in the criticism. It is not caused by anything you did and more importantly, anything you are. Help is available if you choose to escape the drama. Understand that you can't help anyone if you don't take care of yourself first. You are free to choose.

Chapter Two

Family Fights

"I'm Sorry"

There was no moonlight on that dark night, as she crawled across the floor. Knocked down and bruised, she made it a few feet from the door when the next hit to the head stopped her. Bleeding into her ears she heard a voice: "Daddy, don't be mean to Mommy."

The police arrived in time to stop the drunk husband, as he locked his wife in a death-choke while ignoring the pleas of his 3-year-old daughter. This wasn't the first time police had visited the family: in and out of jail for assault, arrested dozens of times, and one more "I'm sorry" as he goes off for a three-year sentence. [12]

Mean-drunk husbands are physically dangerous. Ask any battered wife. Ask any child who has seen the Mr. Hyde-father in action—that is, if they can talk about it. Emotional trauma sometimes has a silencing effect on the suffering-surviving victims.

"It Made Me Observant"

You become very alert when you grow up in a family with a heavy drinker. That's the message from adults who have experienced life with family members who go through life drunk.

Our first Latina Supreme Court Justice grew up in a home with a father who was a heavy drinker: "You become a watchful child. I listened very, very carefully to the world around me to pick up the signals of when trouble was coming. Not that I could stop it. But it made me observant. That was helpful when I became a lawyer, because I know how to read people's signals." [13]

The face shows the change first, before any verbal or physical attack. Another graduate of life in a heavy-drinking home said: "I could tell in an instant when my mother's mood changed. I could see it in her face even when I was a very young child."

As the urge to attack grows, the subtle changes become more obvious. Hostility surfaces in the face: it is a shift to anger, or worse, a sadistic smile of perverse pleasure in anticipation of the attack. It is a shift in intent from kindness, politeness, and civility to cruelty and desire to hurt—meanness.

The mood change is followed by words—cutting, with no rhyme or reason, and containing emotion out of proportion to the meaning of the words spoken. One friend described talking to her mother by phone: "It was like she was killing flies with a sledgehammer."

As another friend described her husband's transformation: "I could see the expression change and I would lie low, trying not to be noticed. It didn't work. He hit me and even shot at me a couple of times. He missed."

These personal stories I hear from my friends are not coming from the bottom rungs of society. These are accomplished professionals who have been the targets of HRA. Why mention that? I think it's important to know that HRA has no social boundaries. It is not restricted to the homeless fighting it out on the street. And it is not always as extreme as getting shot at. HRA is a spectrum of behaviors that touches all strata of society and exists in every country around the world.

I remember a story from the highest levels of finance. It involves a husband and wife who had drinks after spending creative days shaping our financial system's future. Their evening entertainment was arguing and demeaning their only son. They reduced it to a description of "not getting along," with no understanding of the alcohol reaction at the root of their negative family life. These were smart but clueless people, on both the giving and receiving ends of HRA.

Down the road from where I live, a retired doctor killed his wife with a shotgun and used it to commit suicide the same drunken night. They were known to drink heavily and fight often. Neighbors heard loud fighting that night. The bodies were discovered the next day.

"Holding a Beer in His Right Hand"

Over and over we hear the same stories of drunk and abusive husbands and struggling wives. Drunk husbands beat wives—and what is less publicized, drunk wives beat children, or go at them with words of personal condemnation. A friend's mother's weapon of choice was a spatula. When she died, he had a difficult time telling me how things had changed. Finally, he said it as clearly as possible: "The whole family dynamic changed."

Hostility reigns in the land of Mr. Hyde. You must stay alert, because the attack can come from any direction.

Before shooting him with a Taser, the deputy ordered the 21-year-old man to get on the ground. "I again ordered him to get on the ground, and he again did not follow my orders, he instead just looked at me, holding a beer in his right hand." The deputy was there in response to a call from the young man's mother. When the son came home, he asked his mother for the beer he thought she had hidden. She told him he couldn't have more beer because he was already drunk. He became enraged and attacked her. The mother then ran to the bedroom as the son picked up a kitchen knife, which he stabbed into the door. It took three Taser shots before he could be handcuffed. [14]

The hostility reaction to alcohol doesn't make a distinction among relatives. The mother of another son-attacker was not able to make it to safety behind a closed door. Again, the son came home after drinking and claimed his mother got angry, and tried to hit him with a cane, and fell. However, rather than taking her to the hospital, he drove to a friend's house about 30 minutes out of town with his dying mother in the car. He finally made it back to town and the hospital, where his mother was treated for a broken upper-left arm, broken clavicles, and possible internal injuries. The mother said her son hit her. The doctors confirmed he had been drinking. He admitted he had been drinking. His mother died a few hours later.

Two broken collar bones and a broken upper arm point to weapon damage. What could it be? Likely, it was a cane—the same one his mother relied on—the same one he used in a prior attack on her a year earlier, when he was charged with hitting her in the head and arms. This time, he probably whacked her a couple of good ones on both collar bones before she fell. The son was 44 years old. The mother was 74. [15]

"Isn't It Always?"

Recently, my wife and one of our friends, who had just sold her business, were having lunch. During the conversation, our friend said she was considering what to do next. One possibility was to work at a shelter in town for battered women. She had volunteered at shelters where she used to live and had a personal history.

My wife asked: "Didn't you tell me one of your boyfriends beat you?"

"Boyfriend and a husband too."

"Was alcohol involved?"

"Isn't it always?"

It may seem that way for those on the receiving end of the fists but other factors are involved, too. It's life, and people make mistakes and have emotions: jealousy, control issues, insecurities, childhood histories, fear, and anxiety. In life, aren't other emotions always involved any way? These other factors don't necessarily result in violent acts directed toward objects of prior affection. It's the hostile impulse that follows from drinking alcohol that causes the lion's share of damage—verbal and physical.

Alcohol pulls the neurological trigger, which then fires the HRA bullet with intent to hurt or kill, sometimes causing irreparable tragedy. Emotions of all sorts are ever present in any human relationship; but for the alcohol, they likely would be out of public view, remaining private to the parties involved. It's HRA that so often brings otherwise private matters to public view.

"Very Intoxicated"

She dropped her husband off at the bar in the afternoon to meet with three fellow police officers. He arrived back home at night very intoxicated. He got in an argument with her, hit her, grabbed her neck, and pulled her hair, all in front of their two kids.

He said he had been called back to work. Being a police officer herself, she told him there was no way he was going to work drunk, and she didn't believe him anyway. She tried to leave and he wouldn't let her. That was the argument. She went to the bedroom with the kids, and he passed out in the living room. She then took the kids and went to a nearby store to call in the incident. The whole thing was a big mess for everybody involved. [16]

Reason has no home in an incident like this. Remove the alcohol and it might. The people involved might have a chance at communicating and listening to what is important to each other. But alcohol cuts that probability to near zero and drastically increases the likelihood of physical confrontation.

One of the phrases that kept popping up during a research review I made of the admission files at a shelter many years ago captures the problem. It took various forms, but generally went like this: "He kept saying 'Why won't you listen to me?'" Or: "He won't listen to me and he says I won't listen to him." When it comes to couples communicating, "I hear you" is a very important phrase to say and mean. It is the opposite in tone and sentiment to: "She/he won't listen to me." If there was ever a word to be aware of in personal conflicts, *listen* has to be at the top of the list.

HRA makes no class distinctions. It equalizes everyone, from the homeless to police officers to the rich and famous. A New York City news anchor living in Darien, Connecticut with his news anchor wife recently became the news. The husband was arrested and a protective order was issued. He denied hitting and choking his wife. However, while he was at the police station during booking, he announced that he would kill her. Earlier domestic incidents while living in New York City involved his being intoxicated. [17]

Here we have husband and wife police officers, both highly experienced, and a top-tier husband and wife news anchor team making front page news in their respective communities thousands of miles apart, but within days of each other — professional couples caught in the HRA web. Without alcohol, they might have stayed off the front page.

"I Thought That Was What Parents Did — Fight a Lot"

Charlize Theron, an accomplished actress, grew up early and tough, thanks to a strong mother who sent her to boarding school when she was 13. One of the reasons was to protect her from her father. Charlize described him as a good man with a big drinking problem.

When she was 15 and visiting home, Charlize watched her father die. He came home drunk and attacked her mother. He reportedly had a shotgun in hand. Charlize's mother got her own gun and killed him. The shooting was ruled self-defense and no charges were filed.

Recalling her childhood she said: "I just kind of grew up in it. I thought that was what parents did — fight a lot." [18]

If you are young and living in a heavy-drinking home where constant fighting is the normal daily fare, you might wonder how your friends live. Is it the same with their parents?

I was explaining HRA to a friend and his wife during lunch. He got a puzzled look and said, "Isn't it a reaction from drinking alcohol?" Well, it is in the sense that the hostility results *from* drinking. But something happens *to* the brain that is a reaction *to* alcohol — a nasty side effect. It's quite different than the good times and euphoric fun of a party that is usually expected.

Fortunately, at this point my wife spoke up and clarified the concept of HRA. She said, "It is like an allergic reaction to peanuts in some people. It comes from eating peanuts, but the physical danger of a closed airway is a reaction to the peanuts. Some people have this allergic reaction to peanuts. Some people have a hostility reaction to alcohol."

I added, "HRA is a reaction in the brain. It's as if alcohol stimulates a chemical reaction that irritates certain areas of the brain, and hostile behavior results. And while that is going on, alcohol also disrupts the neurotransmission network and the prefrontal cortex that controls the executive functions — such as planning and understanding consequences. The result is loss of rational control over the areas of the brain that involve emotion, fear, and aggression."

Our friend said, "Oh yeah, I remember something that happened when I was living in Texas years ago. I was staying with my sister and we had made friends with a woman from the restaurant. After work one evening, she invited us over for dinner. She was sort of a hefty gal and her husband was real skinny. He said he liked beer and offered me one. After dinner and a lot of beers—at about 2:00 a.m.—I said I had to go home. My sister had left earlier.

"He didn't want me to go, but I had to go to work in a few hours and begged off. He followed me into the parking lot of the apartment complex and started crying. I thought this was a little strange. He said he didn't want me to go and wanted a hug. So I walked up to him and he grabbed me and kneed me in the groin. I pushed back and just watched him as he apologized and said he was sorry. He wanted to give me another hug to show how sorry he was. Not on your life was that going to happen. The whole time he was crying. It's like he was a completely different person than ten minutes ago—he was Jekyll and Hyde.

"That's when I remembered that his wife had told me that he got aggressive when he drank and had tried to beat her up a couple of times. She said she had to knock him down to get him to stop."

This is a good illustration of how the prior attacks on his wife and the subsequent attack on a guest did not originate in something the targets did. Whoever happened to be in front of him when the hostility reaction hit was as good a target as any. Much of our effort to understand alcohol and aggression has focused on what the target of the hostility might have done to provoke the conflict, or which deep-seated emotion triggered the attack—as if reason could explain the cruel drive to hurt a friend or loved one. Reason has nothing to do with it. Look to the hostility reaction caused by alcohol if you want to isolate a cause, and ignore what the Hyde personality tells you to try to justify or excuse the drunken behavior.

"I Have No Idea Why I Did That"

An apartment, a home, and a parking lot are just locations. HRA doesn't care where. Try to beat up your hefty wife one day. Move on to a drinking buddy the next. One target is just as good as the next. This story is similar to one a neighbor told me when we were finishing a morning walk with our dogs. I told him what I was writing about and he volunteered a story from his Navy days.

One night he was in the barracks, and the cook came in after a night of drinking—not uncommon in the Navy. He said he was talking to him about nothing in particular when the cook tried to kick him in the groin—a favorite target for drunks, it seems. My neighbor is a big guy and in good condition and was likely more so back then. His response was to throw the cook around the barracks, banging him into lockers and putting a stop to any chance of a repeat attempt. The next day the cook apologized and said, "I have no idea why I did that—big mistake."

Strange behavior comes from this hostility reaction—vicious verbal and physical attacks, without need of provocation. It comes from within the drinker—from within the brain, and the pathways of the nervous system. The primary intent of HRA is to hurt the target. The last two examples illustrate how impulsive HRA can be. In family life, repeated impulsive attacks on a spouse or child take on an air of intended cruelty, even though little or no planning is involved. However, the hostile intent is unmistakable—planned or not. It's emotion coming from within, even though the drinker attacks with all manner of criticism that seems to blame the target and justify the verbal onslaught.

When the executive functions of mental control and consideration of consequences are overwhelmed by alcohol, all actions seem impulsive. Whether physical or verbal attacks, they are cloaked in the hostile intent to hurt. They are characterized by meanness and lack of consideration for the target or the damage to the relationship. Meanness and displeasure with the supposed inferiority of the target express a clear unhappiness with life. Others seem to be responsible for making the mean drunk happy — if they can't, heads will roll. What a way to go through life.

Fortunately, neuroscience is making progress in understanding the workings of the brain. Alcohol-fueled aggression is being studied, with new evidence pointing to the processes involved in the disruption of the brain's normal functioning. It's the brain, so it's complex. More advances will come — that's the way of good science, building on each insight to create a picture of what exists, and why.

For now, it's enough to acknowledge that the multifaceted variables of genes, neurotransmitters, and brain areas are disrupted by alcohol. [11] We know enough to say that some people have HRA. We can also say that both binge drinking and chronic alcohol consumption increase the probability and intensity of hostility — and we can certainly see the end result in daily life.

HRA is not restrained by age, gender, race, or social status. It is an equal opportunity outcome across all divisions of society and in many countries. It is not an excuse for fighting or murder — it is an explanation.

41

There are several models that describe the contributing factors that surround alcohol and aggression. [11] Ultimately, it boils down to the way alcohol disrupts brain activity to produce aggression, resulting in behavior that hurts or kills.

"He Passed Out Drunk"

The 11-year-old was missing for 25 years. Detectives had a strong suspicion as to what had happened but, lacking sufficient evidence, were unable to make a case. But they never gave up, and the truth eventually surfaced. It took many years, dedicated police work, and new interviews to piece together the facts:

The father admitted to beating his son but denied killing him, saying only that "he passed out drunk and couldn't remember what happened." The victim's sister said she heard the beating going on with screams and thuds and then silence. The aunt said the mother (now dead) told her that the father put the boy's body in the dumpster and waited till the trash was picked up to call police to report that he was missing.

The sister said the boy's father got mad at him for stealing a neighbor's chicken and beat him to death. Here we have a choice of explanations between death because of chicken theft and death because of drunken hostility. Which explanation makes more sense?

No charges were filed for several reasons, including the lack of a body and death of the mother-witness, but the case was solved to the satisfaction of the detectives. [20]

Drunken violence within the family structure hits all members. There is no requirement that limits it to husband against wife or wife against husband, or both against a child.

The one consistent thread is alcohol-caused aggression. Sometimes the attack shows a high degree of impulsivity without a preceding event that could mistakenly be seen as a cause. There is so much alcohol-caused damage in our society that you might think it would be more readily acknowledged. I wonder why it is not. Maybe because too many of us are having too much fun drinking, and making too much money selling this human-aggression fuel.

Alcohol disrupts the flow of signals within the brain. This disruption results in aggression, hostility, and an attempt to dominate. Verbal and physical attacks express the change in brain chemistry. We tend to look for external causes when a mean drunk attacks. Children blame themselves and wonder what they did wrong and how they can change to pacify the attacking parents. Spouses go through the same questioning process, searching for some external reason to explain the emotional chaos. There is no reason in this hostility. It comes from within the drinker—searching externally will never provide a meaningful answer.

So what do we know so far? We know that alcohol affects normal brain activity. A primary outcome is aggression, which we see as a full spectrum of behaviors best described as HRA. This spectrum includes verbal and physical attacks, with as many variations between the two as you can imagine.

We know that blackouts are very common, even among social drinkers. Blackouts can be both partial and complete—the more alcohol and the faster the consumption, the greater the memory impairment. New memories are simply not formed, due to disruption of the brain area central to autobiographical memory — the hippocampus. [9]

We know from experimental studies that "alcohol does indeed cause aggression." This is the conclusion of an exhaustive meta-analysis specifically designed to eliminate any question that causation was being confused with correlation. This landmark review established the causal link between drinking and aggression in a way that eliminated past arguments to the contrary. [10]

We know now that "violent behavior is much more common in alcohol-dependent individuals." This is one of the conclusions of a recent review study that deals with the complex challenge in achieving neurobiological understanding of the mechanisms involved in HRA. "These studies have shown that environmental factors, such as early-life stress, interact with genetic variations in serotonin-related genes that affect serotonergic and GABAergic neurotransmission. This leads to increased alcohol intake and impulsive aggression. In addition, acute and chronic alcohol intake can further impair executive control and thereby facilitate aggressive behavior." [11]

The three review studies noted above are the result of much work over many years by many researchers doing hundreds of specific studies. It's not like this issue has been neglected by the academic community. Nor is it a mystery in the law enforcement community, in emergency rooms, and on airlines. Alcohol-fueled belligerence in those arenas is well known. Yet there is still a lack of awareness by the public — a lingering expectation of only happy times for all who drink — with little understanding of the dark side, unless touched personally.

Chapter Three

The Cause

"How Could You Do This to a Kid?"

"We would walk around on eggshells all day. I remember playing around the house. If something would break, it didn't matter what kid it was, we all had to line up, drop pants, and he would just whip us. I remember not being able to sit for a week at a time, just in so much pain."

It was a rough life for this young man and his family. His father was a heavy drinker and they were homeless much of the time. This was a family of five kids held together by a determined mother.

When he was in college the son confronted his father about the beatings he and his four siblings received over the years. He asked: "How could you do this to a kid? To five kids?" The father finally accepted responsibility after he quit drinking, and explained that alcohol had taken over his life. The son forgave him and now they have a good relationship.

So, redemption is possible. It's difficult to take responsibility, of course, but having the strength to get help and get into recovery is the first step. This particular redemption and reconciliation happened because the father made it to recovery, stopped drinking, and as a result gained his son's respect. [21]

To understand what is happening here, we need to know what happens in the brain that would make a father line up his five children and beat them. Breaking something is not the cause. It may be used as justification by the father, but it is not the cause; nor is it a suitable explanation of why he beat his children.

"Jealousy Motive Suspected"

It's a strange feeling when you have a basic understanding of HRA and see a headline that says "Jealousy Motive Suspected in Death" and you know that the story will involve drinking by both parties. [23] A more accurate headline might read: "Woman Killed by Friend in Drunken Rage." What was the motivation—the cause?

Certain aspects of alcohol-fueled aggression become obvious when you understand the basic behaviors that flow from it. Hostility is hard to miss, but often there's also an alcohol-inspired feeling that is mistaken for power and courage preceding aggression. This is what allows a small man to impulsively attack someone who is sure to throw him across the room. Jealousy is another feeling spurred by drinking.

The standard crime-solving framework of motive, means, and opportunity works well as a simple method for solving many murders. But as we grow in our knowledge of human behavior, we need more. We want a deeper understanding of what causes us to be the way we are.

We are always looking for something other than alcohol to excuse or explain drunken behavior, to the point of ignoring its role in daily tragedy. By now, it must be reasonably clear that alcohol is an accurate explanation for certain inflamed passions and hostile behavior. Explanation does not equal excuse. Explanation is a step toward understanding, truth, and responsibility.

Feelings and emotions resulting from changes in the brain often are expressed as observable behaviors. Ultimately, it's important to determine what changes occur in the brain to produce hostile aggression.

Breaking Out of Limiting Frameworks

At one time, the prevailing view of the social science community was that no evidence existed proving that alcohol causes aggression. This view dominated for years, in the face of all experience to the contrary. Thankfully, enough studies using accepted scientific methods have been completed to end that assertion.

Now, the challenge to understanding human behavior involves scientists who study how the brain works. Neuroscience is becoming increasingly effective in determining the underlying neurobiological causes of human behavior, with help from advances in technology.

Functional MRI imaging allows us to see areas of the brain as they are being used. The isolation of new molecules that influence behavior also has opened doors to further understanding. Our challenge is to frame current progress in a way that clarifies understanding of drinking and the aggression that follows.

As laymen who want to understand, we need a flexible framework to apply to human behavior, consistent with both daily life and scientific knowledge.

The premise of this book is that hostile behavior following drinking is the result of biochemical changes in the brain, triggered by alcohol. Alcohol stimulates a neurochemical that irritates areas of the brain associated with aggression. This causes some people to be increasingly irritable, angry, and hostile the more they drink. This hostility reaction happens in certain contexts, such as homes, bars, and parties, and airplanes. The hostile behavior that follows drinking produces consequences. These alcohol-fueled consequences often reach far beyond the obvious arguments and fights that we have touched on so far. We can say that HRA involves:

Cause
Context
Consequence

All three parts of this framework are complex, with multiple variables, but we can simplify them. For example, we can say the *cause* of HRA is a change in brain chemistry and leave it at that (but we won't); we can say that it occurs in a *context*, involving external factors—family life, commonly known as domestic violence (as well as many other contexts); and we can say there are *consequences* for those involved—ruined relationships, death, criminal prosecution, costs to society, and more.

Let's start by looking for a possible neurobiological cause. What does science know that might explain the neurochemistry of HRA? What is the single most likely cause, based on the currently available science? And can we accept today's science, with the proviso that new discoveries will follow to more fully clarify what we know? We are looking for high probability, not certainty. We are looking for clues in current neurological studies that solve the mystery with as high a degree of certainty as possible, knowing that scientific advances will add to our understanding in ways we can't imagine today.

With those thoughts in mind, I will take a stab at defining the cause of HRA.

The Missing Link

HRA is a neurological response to alcohol. It occurs in the brain and causes aggressive behavior in certain contexts, often with serious consequences. This might seem like a statement of the obvious, but the scientific basis of social progress these days requires something more specific: for example, wouldn't it be useful to know which molecule or family of molecules is causing all the trouble? Maybe the answer is staring us in the face and we've missed the connection, until now. One candidate holds promise.

In the November 2006 issue of *Brain, Behavior, and Immunity,* Steven Zalcman and Allan Siegel of UMDNJ-New Jersey Medical School published a report stating:

"Recent studies have suggested an important relationship linking cytokines, immunity and aggressive behavior. Clinical reports describe increasing levels of hostility, anger, and irritability in patients who receive cytokine immunotherapy, and there are reports of a positive correlation between cytokine levels and aggressive behavior in non-patient populations." [24]

What caught my attention in the report was the mention of "hostility, anger, and irritability in patients." I substituted "heavy drinkers" for "patients" and saw the possibility of finding the neurochemical cause of HRA.

The next step was to find a relationship between cytokines and alcohol. It wasn't difficult. In the April 2006 issue of *Alcoholism: Clinical and Experimental Research*, F. T. Crews et al. published a review report, "Cytokines and Alcohol," which stated in part:

"Cytokines are multifunctional proteins that play a critical role in cellular communication and activation."

"Cytokines affect the brain and likely contribute to changes in the central nervous system that contribute to long-term changes in behavior and neurodegeneration. Together these studies suggest that ethanol disruption of cytokines and inflammation contribute in multiple ways to a diversity of alcoholic pathologies." [25]

Next, I discovered that the relationship between cytokines and alcohol is a subject of growing interest to researchers. The key to understanding what is happening is that alcohol triggers the release of cytokines within the body, including the brain. In a 2010 study, circulating cytokines were found to be a possible biomarker of alcohol abuse:

"This is an emerging and potentially exciting avenue of research in that circulating cytokines may contribute to diagnostic biomarker panels and a combination of multiple biomarkers may significantly increase the sensitivity and specificity of the biochemical tests aiding reliable and accurate detection of excessive alcohol intake." [28]

The inflamed passions of hostility, anger, and irritability from drinking are linked in the brain by cytokines. These little molecules may be the missing link between alcohol and aggression—a molecular bridge within the brain.

Alcohol is a toxin—think intoxication—that elicits a protective response within the brain. As part of the process, brain cells in areas associated with aggression and rage are signaled by cytokines to take action, triggering hostility, anger, and irritability. The more alcohol consumed in a given time, the greater the production of cytokines and the greater the likelihood that hostility and blackouts will result. The whole process is an automatic physical reaction to alcohol by the body, including the brain.

It's most simply described as inflammation. Cytokines can be either proinflammatory or anti-inflammatory. They function as part of the immune system when the body, including the brain, is invaded by a threat, such as an infection. Their job is to isolate the intruder and protect the host. But they can get out of balance and do a lot of damage.

Alcohol is a physical threat. Prolonged drinking increases damage to the liver, brain, and much more. It's understandable that a drinker's defense mechanisms would produce cytokines in response to alcohol, signaling cells to protect. This disruption of the cytokine defense mechanism causes multiple and confusing problems for the body. [30]

Hostility, anger, and irritability increase as the cell-signaling cytokines in the brain seem to urge the drinker to fight back. This is an automatic cellular process, which is why the attack behavior is beyond our ability to understand using reason when we focus only on the context and consequences of the hostility.

Cytokines are produced as part of an immune response in a defensive attempt to protect against alcohol. HRA is an unfortunate byproduct of this attempt. The hostility and the personality traits characteristic of this reaction are basically the same for all heavy drinkers subject to it. However, the intensity of HRA varies among individuals, raising the likelihood that genetic expression and neurosystem differences between individuals play an important role. Murderous violence and verbal demeaning form the bookends of this spectrum, with many stories between the two.

This complex process is part of the immune system and is a type of neuroinflammation. [31]

The motive of a drunk father who lines up his five children for a sequential beating has the same link. The brutal beatings, the verbal attacks, and the drama of drinking life are linked to the imbalance of cytokines, which signal regions of the brain associated with aggression. The release of cytokines is a protective reaction to the perceived threat of alcohol.

Knowing that inflammation is the cause of the hostility puts the context and consequence of HRA in perspective. For example, you now can understand that the cause of the family argument is unrelated to the details of the context, which are often cited as an excuse for the fighting and verbal abuse. Context and consequences are important, but fall far short of an explanation. Explanation can come only from understanding the neurobiological cause — inflammation in specific areas of the brain.

For example, I was driving to work one morning years ago and noticed five police cars at the house of a woman who, many years earlier, had been a member of my high school class. The next day, I found out what happened. She and her boyfriend had spent the night before drinking beer. During this last night of her life, she pulled a photo album from the bookcase and the two sat on the couch looking at pictures of her past. At some point he became jealous, went into the kitchen, came back with a knife, and stabbed her to death.

He has to live with what he did, and she is dead. How should we explain what happened?

Cause, context, and consequence separate the chaos into an understandable framework: the cause is HRA; the context is the home; the consequence is murder. Why complicate it? But wasn't jealousy at least some form of catalyst or contributing factor? I wouldn't argue with that. But people get jealous all the time without killing reactively because of things that happened long before the jealous one arrived on the scene. There is always an initial catalyst—usually described as an argument—that precedes the eruption of drunken violence; but it is not the *cause* of the consequence.

Jealousy is part of the complex of human emotions. It is a major factor in human relations and shouldn't be minimized. But in this case, alcohol-caused inflammation was in control, not a passing sense of jealousy. [32] The link with jealousy must take second place. To say jealousy is the cause is like saying anger is the cause, both of which imply a transfer of blame to the victim for causing the emotion in the attacker. It's this type of superficial dismissal of human interaction that prevents learning. If we are ever to progress as humans, we must move beyond the obvious emotions of daily life. There are scientific explanations that clarify the tragedies we visit on each other. As science progresses, we progress. It's our best chance of coping with ourselves.

Knowing that this chaos is caused by inflammation of specific areas of the brain provides you with a coping skill. When you see HRA click in, you can step back and evaluate the potential for escalation and violence. If you are being criticized by a family member over a holiday dinner, you can cope by acknowledging, maybe only silently to yourself, that the criticism is a reaction caused by alcohol. Understanding the cause can give you the ability to cope as the situation requires.

Reconciling Cause and Responsibility

Knowing the cause does not remove personal responsibility. Someone who is drunk and beats his wife to death is no less responsible than a drunk driver who drives the wrong way on the freeway and kills an entire family in a head-on collision.

This may seem self-evident, but there is public resistance to, and denial of, the causal relationship between alcohol and violent behavior. Part of the problem is the lack of widespread knowledge of the science behind the alcohol-violence causal relationship. The other part is fear that if alcohol were ever acknowledged as a cause, it would lead the legal system to excuse the criminal because of alcohol use. Worse, alcohol eventually would be accepted as a defense, removing responsibility from the guilty. This is a false fear. It has not happened with drunk drivers, who routinely are convicted.

Knowing the irresponsibility and danger of driving drunk has increased the severity of social condemnation and punishment, placing responsibility on the driver. But to get to this point, it took a concerted effort by organizations such as Mothers Against Drunk Driving pushing against the liquor lobbies in state legislatures to strengthen laws.

Lack of knowledge of the causal relationship between alcohol and violence is a major hurdle facing society. We may have to go through the same process we did with driving drunk to achieve public awareness of HRA. Eventually, there may be broad acceptance that alcohol disrupts and disturbs. It disrupts the neurosystem and disturbs behavior. And the leading candidate for causing the trouble is a cytokine system that is knocked off balance by alcohol, producing inflammation in the areas of the brain associated with aggression.

The Eyes Don't See What the Mind Doesn't Know

Sometimes it's difficult to believe what you're seeing. With enough experience, seeing and believing can come together with meaning and clarity. I remember walking with a friend when I was about 12 years old. We entered his back yard and noticed that the chickens had just escaped the coop. There were about 20 hens, leaving calmly through a gate that had somehow opened itself.

In an attempt to encourage them to retreat, my friend picked up a rock and lobbed it toward the flock. As fate would have it, the rock connected dead-on with the little head of a hapless hen, who went down, out cold. What happened next was a scene out of an unmade Hitchcock film. The 19 upright chickens immediately rushed to the downed bird with a fury of pecking that you had to see to believe. Attacking brought them together and allowed us herd them into the pen, saving the flattened hen from further damage. She eventually recovered and continued producing eggs.

What does this have to do with the subject of drinkers who become hostile? In a way, it's similar to behavior that often involves pecking at, or picking on, those unable or unwilling to fight back—the vulnerable.

Little verbal jabs disguised as some worthy purpose, perhaps as a wish to help the target become the person the pecking drinker thinks she should be. It's difficult to see pecking that is so frequent, skillful, and manipulative as to be barely distinguishable from the literal meaning of the words that give form to the attack. It's difficult to separate the hostility from the demeaning words of blame.

But there is a less obvious force at work as well. The chickens were involved in pattern behavior—an automatic, reactive attack on the vulnerable. So is the hostile drunk who belittles and maligns a vulnerable target. It's pattern behavior. The predictable attack by a drunk, often involving the same criticisms of prior attacks, is similar to the mindless attack of the chickens.

Anyone who has experienced daily contact with drunken hostility knows how incessantly persistent and repetitive it is. Keep in mind that a demeaning phone call works just as effectively as a face-to-face conversation.

But learning to see what is happening takes practice and thought. A good friend once told me that a professor in medical school kept drumming into him that "the eyes don't see what the mind doesn't know." That statement captures the challenge to awareness when you first try to understand the drama of irritation, anger, and hostility that is the consequence of drinking. To see the cause is difficult when you are immersed in the context of the turmoil and living the consequences every day. However, there is a lot to see when the mind knows what to look for.

Facilitate your understanding by looking behind the words to the repetitive pecking— the automatic, unaware, and unthinking urge of the drinker. Remember that you are dealing with a disrupted neural network and the disturbed personality that results, which is compelled and driven to pick on the vulnerable. You can learn to see, even if the drinker is totally unaware. Watch for the peck, peck, peck. It's part of the HRA behavioral spectrum. It's inflammation in action.

Explosive physical violence is at the other end of the spectrum. My older son and a friend were returning from the mountains after a day of snow boarding on a snow-packed icy day. They stopped at a convenience store on the way home. In the iced-over parking lot, two very inebriated guys were arguing and pushing each other. Suddenly one slipped and fell, and the other straddled him and started slamming his head against the pavement. It was awful, vicious, and sudden. Then just as suddenly he stopped, cradled the unconscious in his arms, crying and shouting, "My friend, my friend." That's how the inflammation of HRA works in real life.

There is no happiness in these dramas of drinking and anger: from macho-drinker to bully-father; from party girl to scolding wife; and friends who slip on the ice. All are suffering-surviving members of the HRA club. They are all experiencing the cytokine agents of hostility that roam the brain, inflaming passions, creating misery, and spreading conflict among all involved. This brain inflammation process is probably a stone age survival mechanism designed to put an end to a real danger. When it is triggered by alcohol, all it does is cause trouble.

Defensive action is a response to a threat. The immune system reacts automatically to the toxic threat of damage posed by alcohol. This defensive immune response releases cytokines in the body and brain in an attempt to counteract the toxin. Certain proinflammatory cytokines signal cells in the parts of the brain associated with the activation of defensive aggression. The unfortunate result is one or more of the behaviors that express HRA. While we don't yet know the exact neuromechanism, this is the basic inflammation process involved in HRA.

When you know the cause of the drama, you have the potential to gain a degree of understanding and objectivity. Knowing that you are facing a molecule at work that is part of the immune system can give you strength to deal with the hostility, anger, and irritability. One little cell-signaling troublemaker may be at the root of the problem—and possibly at the root of much other alcohol-related pathology.

When you read a news article that involves senseless beatings and murder, ask yourself if your eyes see what your mind knows. Look behind the superficial report and consider the probability that HRA played a causal role. Look at the context. Was it late at night? Was it in an area with bars where drinkers collect, expecting fun and laughter? Have you ever received a late-night phone call from a lone drinker, expressing unhappiness with the behavior of a selected target—complaining, demeaning, criticizing? What caused that call?

Do you know an aging drinker who has nothing good to say about anyone, any issue, any news event? What is causing the negativity?

The depression and negative life view that so often accompany chronic drinking are clues that proinflammatory cytokines are being released. The simplest way to describe this process is to say that alcohol causes inflammation of the brain areas associated with aggression, producing hostility. When you understand, you can make new choices, no matter which side of the hostility threshold you happen to be on at the time.

Chapter Four

Celebrities at Play

"I Am Deeply Embarrassed"

Your personality changes when you drink a lot. You lose your unique humanity and enter the world of so many who have gone before you. Mean and hostile drinkers go through life with cookie-cutter personalities, scaring the vulnerable.

The more you drink, the more damage you do to your brain and the less like yourself you become. Your Hyde personality is not an individual moving through life in happiness. You are the same as all the other Hyde personalities who came before you and all that will come after you. Who is the real you — without the alcohol?

No matter how rich or famous or privileged you are, you can become part of the cookie-cutter personality parade. All it takes is enough alcohol to cause it and the right context to support it, and the consequences follow with ease.

The rich and famous are in the news as much as the poor and unknown when it comes to alcohol and hostility — and they are often as surprised by the consequences of their actions as are their fans.

As Reese Witherspoon said after her husband was pulled over for DUI with her as a passenger and arrested, sitting in the back of the squad car: "What have I done? What did I get arrested for?" It took her husband to explain to her that she had interfered with the arresting officer: "He told you to stop. You wouldn't listen to what he said."

Listening is often a challenge when sober, but more difficult when drunk. Even after being arrested for arguing with a police officer Reese continued quizzing her drunken husband for clarification and arguing: "I'm an American citizen. I can say whatever I want to on free ground. He does not have jurisdiction over the ground he speaks on. He does not. I'm allowed to say anything I want to say." Cognitive impairment and poor judgment ruled in this case. A partial blackout was likely. HRA was not in doubt.

Reese's husband crossed the center line, which led to his being stopped. He got out of the car and failed the sobriety test, standing quietly while Reese, disobeying the police officer, got out of the car and chose the wrong time and place to exercise her First Amendment rights to free speech and advocacy.

In a statement released in the sober light of the Sunday after Thursday's arrest she explained:

"I clearly had one drink too many and I am deeply embarrassed about the things I said. It was definitely a scary situation and I was frightened for my husband, but that is no excuse. I was disrespectful to the officer who was just doing his job. I have nothing but respect for the police and I'm very sorry for my behavior." [35]

What a contrast from the drunk and disorderly to the polite, real Reese. The statement that she was frightened for her husband contains a clue to the activity in her brain. She sensed a threat in her drunken state and responded with all the hostility her disrupted and inflamed system could muster—the cause. The context of the confrontation did not bode well for the consequences that she might have expected when she let the officer know she was a celebrity. She asked him if he knew her name while she was being cuffed. He said he didn't want to know right then.

Not much reasoning was involved in her attempt to control the situation. When she was sitting in the back of the patrol car, asking her husband why they were being arrested and what she did wrong, she apparently didn't realize what she had done—or maybe didn't remember. Not unusual for a disrupted neurosystem that produces disturbed behavior.

Reese was compelled to take action—to get out of the car and confront the officer; she couldn't help herself. This is the underlying aggression—the urge of HRA. Not only does the drunk feel hostile, angry, and irritated, but also righteous and courageous when faced with a perceived threat. This compulsion is aggression, supported by the indignation of intoxication and the doubt-free certainty that only intoxicated confidence can provide.

Compulsion is what hostile aggression feels like. Hostility is the manifestation of that aggression in a form intended to put down another person verbally or physically. It's crucial to make a distinction between the urge that compels the drunk to act in pursuit of conflict and the hostile behavior that follows. It's an important difference when trying to understand the dynamics of drunken behavior.

You might wonder what kind of threat being pulled over by a police officer is for a famous celebrity. It's a threat to the ego. "How dare a public servant infringe on my life. Doesn't he know who I am?" Of course, Reese didn't say that, but she implied it when she asked if he knew her name. And she was compelled to defend herself — her ego.

If you're drunk, you don't have to be famous to experience the inflated ego of intoxication. It's well known in the drinking literature. [36] An inflated ego might be one of the byproducts of inflammation and the resulting attempt to protect — to build up confidence for a fight. The feeling of superiority and the compulsion to make all others inferior by belittling are part of the spectrum of HRA behaviors. The process of maligning inflates the ego by making others seem less worthy than the all-knowing and all-judging drunk.

Confidence, courage, and a sense of superiority describe the feelings that come with the aggression generated by alcohol. Remember Mike Wallace's description of Johnny Carson as feeling able to take on the Russian army. This unfounded, imaginary confidence could be part of the protective action of cytokines signaling the brain, trying to give the drinker the tools (aggressive confidence, courage, and strength) necessary to fight the physical threat of alcohol. This is not so far-fetched if you remember that we are dealing with disruption of the brain, resulting in the aberrant behavior we call drunkenness. In a sense, this is a product of the immune system trying to protect the drinker by releasing cytokines that cause brain inflammation.

The problem is that it's counterproductive from a health standpoint because it reinforces drinking and places the drinker in situations that any sober person would avoid. As the drinking continues, the feeling of superiority and control grows. To express this feeling of aggressive strength and false courage, the drinker is compelled to criticize and insult others. The individual personality is lost, replaced by negative and aggressively hostile stereotypical behavior, designed to hurt.

The time spent drinking and the amount of alcohol needed for cytokines to inflame the brain and activate hostile aggression differs for each of us. For Johnny Carson, it was instant. For Reese Witherspoon, it was a night on the town. Both saw the problem and escaped before it was too late. How many ordinary lives are shaped by egos built up by alcohol? How widespread is this distortion of reality? Or is this just the world we have created by drinking through the centuries of human history?

"Alcoholic Rages"

Liza Minnelli and David Gest were married for about a year before they filed for divorce. There was a lot of fighting over money—as is to be expected in high society—and the court proceedings made for sensational news headlines.

During this divorce war, Gest filed a suit claiming that he was injured because Minnelli "beat him so bad during alcoholic rages that he had to be hospitalized." Apparently he was suffering from headaches. Her expert witness said the headaches were not from the beatings, but from a virus. His doctor said they were caused by the beatings and that he tested negative for the virus. The judge threw out the case. [19]

There is always drama surrounding heavy drinking. Sometimes it's as if the drunken expression of emotion is an attempt to justify the aggression and hostility. But that's probably giving too much credit for rational thought to the drunk.

Tonya Harding, the skater, is remembered for her association with a knee bashing incident during the 1994 Olympics, which resulted in her being banned from skating for hindering the investigation. Some years ago, she had her own public run-in with HRA. According to the police, she was arrested for smashing her boyfriend's face with a hubcap in a drunken rage. "Drunken rage" is such a useful and frequent description. It's right up there with getting kneed in the groin, which is what her boyfriend claimed she did to him.

Police reported that both were drunk; Harding was staggering around, speaking loudly and slurring her words. Earlier, she said her boyfriend had forced her to defend herself. [41]

Witnesses said Harding started punching as soon as they got out of the car. Her boyfriend just let her hit him, eventually grabbing her arms. Perhaps that's when the knee went into action—nasty business, these alcoholic rages. Although useful, rage is a description that falls short and is accepted without question as the cause when it's actually an expression of the underlying neurological cause.

One friend described her experience at a dinner party. A retired financial executive from the East stood out—and by all indications that's exactly what he intended. As our friend described the scene, you could always tell where he was in the room because most of the group was somewhere else. "He was full of himself and became increasingly insulting the more he drank." Her husband added: "He comes to the party drunk and gets drunker." Why would anyone want to be around him if all he does is issue insults?

We had friends over for dinner recently, and the subject of HRA came up. The description of one woman's experience was instructive. She told how she became argumentative and overconfident when she drank; she had relatives who became nasty, and a former boyfriend who hit her. She was experienced in observing HRA in several contexts, with different consequences. It made me think how widespread the hostility reaction is. It seems very common and a primary risk of drinking. With the right amount of time and alcohol, it can intrude on any life.

Watching her describe the moment her boyfriend's face changed and how at that moment she knew he would hit her was better than any academic study. She said it was like a switch being turned on. While she was talking and reliving the experience, I was thinking how her boyfriend's cytokines were activating the brain areas associated with aggression and starting to send signals — it's time to attack.

Strange what you can imagine when you know that inflammation is spreading in the brain. Remember, this type of neuroinflammation is the action of proinflammatory cytokines working on the brain to initiate hostile behavior, and sometimes erase any memory of what happened, all done as part of the immune system reacting to the toxin alcohol.

Reading facial changes is one of the first things abused children learn. It's no different for abused adults heading for the battered women's shelters. That's when the fear starts — when you see the face change. [40]

It must be difficult for people without direct experience to realize that facial changes are significant indicators of the hostile aggression to come. But when you gain awareness from repeated real-life experience, it can come in handy and give you the first clue to avoid a situation.

"Booze Makes Him a Different Person"

For years, Mel Gibson has fought an affinity for alcohol. His arrest for driving drunk and the behavior that followed is a textbook example of the hostility reaction in action.

After being stopped for driving drunk, he began a tirade of cursing and demeaning insults that illustrate the Hyde personality. His invective spanned the globe, with anti-Semitic blame attached. In the police station, he continued with comments directed at selected officers — not the best choice for insults when being arrested.

At the initial arrest stop, he refused to get in the patrol car and ran. The deputy caught and cuffed him, put him in the car, and listened to his rant on the drive to the station. Being a good deputy, his report detailed the insulting comments Mel made during the ride and at the station. The report was thorough. The insults were so hate-filled that a superior officer asked the deputy to clean it up because it was "way too inflammatory."

This is inflammation in the brain, followed by an inflammatory gush of words, demonstrating HRA in full fury. Mel yelled words that reflected fear for his image and reputation because of the arrest — his ego and public image were threatened. This hostility was part of the brain's inflamed attempt to deal with that perceived threat, based on a strategy distorted by a drunken lack of reason.

He issued a statement shortly after his ordeal:

"After drinking alcohol on Thursday night, I did a number of things that were very wrong and for which I am ashamed. I drove a car when I should not have, and was stopped by the LA County Sheriffs. The arresting officer was just doing his job and I feel fortunate that I was apprehended before I caused injury to any other person. I acted like a person completely out of control when I was arrested, and said things that I do not believe to be true and which are despicable. I am deeply ashamed of everything I said. Also, I take this opportunity to apologize to the deputies involved for my belligerent behavior. They have always been there for me in my community and indeed probably saved me from myself. I disgraced myself and my family with my behavior and for that I am truly sorry. I have battled with the disease of alcoholism for all of my adult life and profoundly regret my horrific relapse. I apologize for any behavior unbecoming of me in my inebriated state and have already taken necessary steps to ensure my return to health." [37]

Mel's friends stood by him. They made statements that clearly separated his two personalities, one drunk and one sober. Apparently, he has a well-defined Jekyll and Hyde personality that they describe as: "Booze makes him a different person." He's not the only one, but the extremes were obvious in his case.

Although they differed in intensity, the similarity in Reese's brush with the law and Mel's reflect the cookie-cutter nature of drunken hostility in the context of being a celebrity: The compulsion to talk, the perceived threat, the anger and insulting behavior toward the arresting officers, and the apologetic press release are a pattern that points to the same cause.

Sometimes it's helpful to look at extreme behavior to appreciate everyday, routine hostility. Most drunken fights are probably hidden and unreported. There are no reliable statistics that reflect the damage. Until now, there was no name for what we call the hostility reaction to alcohol—HRA. And there certainly was no understanding that it stemmed from inflammation in the brain caused by the immune system responding to the toxic effects of alcohol. But we are making progress and beginning to understand the complex details of this damaging chemical on the behavior of heavy drinkers.

"Kneed an Officer"

Glen Campbell had a collision in Phoenix, drove off, and was followed to his home by a witness. When the police arrived, he was tested for his blood-alcohol content, which was so high that he was charged with extreme drunken driving.

He was booked and was minutes away from being released on bail when out of the blue he kneed an officer in the thigh—so drunk he missed the usual target. The report said he became angry and let go with the knee. Anger is the reason of record for doing something so obviously stupid. But as we know, this type of impulsive knee-attack is a common expression of HRA. In this case, it added an assault charge to Campbell's record.

But it didn't end there. As the police reported: "There was a lot of, 'Do you know who I am? I'm Glen Campbell...I shouldn't be locked up like this.'" He also demanded to see the police chief. So he went from drunk driving to assaulting an officer, along with the entire: "Do you know who I am" verbiage of an arrested celebrity ego.

If you want to see an example of the face of Hyde, check out Glen Campbell's booking photo on the Internet. Remember that this photo was taken before the kneeing episode, when the personality change was in full force. Shortly after the mug shot, the anger bubbled to the surface and the physical attack followed. Why would anyone moments away from being released, after being booked, knee an officer? There is only one correct answer to this question.

His statement contained the standard apology:

"Yesterday I was arrested and put in jail. Even at my age, I learned a valuable lesson. I apologize to my wife, my family, and my fans." [38]

Country western singers seem to have a muse in alcohol. It is part of the life until it gets so bad that it just can't go on anymore. Randy Travis went through it, as did George Jones. Alcohol seems to go with the failed marriages and hard life on the road.

Life's tragedies often precede a reach for the bottle. In George Jones's case, he first saw what it was all about when his father started drinking after the death of his sister. As he wrote in his autobiography, he was loved when his father was sober, but a prisoner when he was drunk. He learned early.

Perhaps it was the genetic call that made it easy for George to drink through his singing success—tearing up hotel rooms and getting into fistfights as one hit song after another carried him into the 1960s. After several visits to rehab, he was able to limit his drinking, with several relapses. [39] It almost seems that alcohol has been the source of much of the sadness typical of country-western music.

An out-of-control ego is often a clue that you are dealing with someone who might have a serious drinking problem. Certainly you don't have to be drunk to exhibit an inflated ego. Power and control over another is the perfect context for constant belittling, and often it doesn't involve alcohol. But when you see aggressive dominance, try to expand your perspective and consider the possibility that alcohol may be involved. Certainly, this is the situation with a heavy-drinking parent who demeans her children and husband. It's also the case with chronically intoxicated men who abuse the women in their lives.

What is less obvious is that the same cookie-cutter behavior is in play in the business world. Here is where the importance of alcohol tolerance becomes apparent. Here is where the impulses of power and control from chronic brain inflammation hide behind authority, maligning others and expressing the drunken ego with impunity. Tolerance for alcohol is a prerequisite in this context. The executive in power can't be falling-down drunk or even slurring words, which makes it all the more difficult to accept that HRA is behind the abuse. But in some cases, it's easy to follow the hostility back to the alcohol.

Imagine sitting in a board of directors' morning meeting when one of the members has been out all night drinking and chooses to dominate the gathering by insulting the chairman and everything he proposes—for hours. Why would he do such a negative, unproductive thing?

Imagine sitting around a table having drinks after a successful conference when the leader of the whole operation starts in on the second in command, criticizing his every action and reason for being, his eyes closed to narrow slits and his mouth distorted in an expression that can only be described as evil. This type of scene is difficult to watch and even more difficult for the second in command.

There are irritable, angry, and hostile executives who run businesses and make a practice of insulting the vulnerable who depend on them for a livelihood. This is a different context than the abuse found in a home with a chronic drinker. But the abuse is no less harmful for those targeted, and the cause is the same.

It's also the same "do you know who I am behavior" of a celebrity, but without a police officer to put on the cuffs. There is not going to be a carefully worded press-release apology the following day. These are people who are legends in their own minds, with no higher authority to stop them.

There is no law against verbally abusing colleagues that will land a powerful executive in jail. In the cases cited above, the board member was obviously under the influence. The leader at the end of the conference was less obvious, but possibly more instructive: For example, he had an inflated ego and was making false accusations directed toward one of the people at the table—both classic signs of chronic drinking. [36] But the inescapable sign was his hostile aggression and the face of Hyde that went with it. Here is where there is no escaping the signs of brain inflammation caused by chronic drinking. It shows in the face and in the belittling of others. Keep in mind that wine works as well as beer, and hard liquor tops them all.

Why is it important to develop awareness of this type of attack behavior? In these examples, the executives were judging whoever happened to be in front of them. So, you might want to question their judgment—especially if you are the one being judged. Brain inflammation distorts judgment, and the words that follow are reactions to the inflammation rather than generated by reason and informed by the situation at hand. The rudeness and bullying are reactions to alcohol. It is not really about the target of the attack. It's pitiful when you understand what's behind all the bravado.

Also, remember that tolerance for alcohol is one sign of a chronic drinker. We tend not even to consider that a person might be under the influence unless he or she is glass-eyed-wasted and slurring words or staggering. This stereotype of a drunk is misleading. Many are articulate, incisive, and self-directed. Sometimes the only obvious and reliable sign is the hostility toward other people.

Perhaps in the future, a majority of us will understand HRA and the brain inflammation that causes it. When that day comes, pushing back against abuse with a scientific understanding of HRA could be routine. For example, standing up from the judgment table and informing the drinker that he has no right to talk to you that way, and that it must never happen again is a start. If history is any guide, he will look at you in wonderment with no idea of what you are talking about.

Nevertheless, knowing the cause increases the chance of overcoming the hurt of a drunken attack. It's easier to explain something to a chronic drinker when you have the clarity of truth working for you. But you might want to wait for a moment of sobriety before taking on the task. Even then, the chance of imposing awareness is probably a long shot. Awareness almost always has to come from within, and with time.

Keep in mind that there is always hope. There are alternatives, even though none of them may be easy. The board member in the example above actually stopped drinking and became a positive contributor to the organization. The transformation was in stark contrast to his past drinking persona, much to the relief of his colleagues. He stopped through his own awareness, and by choice. The leader who had drinks after a successful conference shows no awareness of his behavior.

Admiration is warranted when people take hold of their lives and change for their own sake and those around them. Celebrities are good examples for understanding the difficulties of life and how to overcome them because their problems are often public. In many cases they are open, or forced to be open, about both the good and the bad.

Some years back, Jamie Lee Curtis was interviewed on the TV show Entertainment Tonight. It was like Johnny Carson all over again. Her statement was so casual and matter-of-fact, but reflected such awareness and power of choice that you have to admire her—especially when you know how difficult it is for many others to do the same.

Jamie Lee said she stopped drinking because she realized it was a factor in fights with her 13 year-old adopted daughter. [42] Self-awareness and responsibility led Jamie Lee to choose not to drink. She realized the effect that alcohol had on her personality and the danger it posed for her and her daughter, and she made a choice. To drink or not drink is always a personal choice. So is getting help to stop if you need it.

Chapter Five

Confined Conflict

"I Don't Know Why She Became So Angry"

It's natural to attribute the cause of an event to the context. Context is what we see initially, and we tend to look at a particular location for explanations, or at least as a way of describing what happened. But the location of drunken violence is not the cause—it's the context. The air rage of a passenger out of control, an ER patient erupting with hostility, or a violent bar fight are all conflicts within different contexts.

Contexts are not the cause of the hostile aggression that so often follows drinking. This is an important distinction. Attributing cause based on context obscures understanding. When we name something without understanding the cause, important elements get filed away and forgotten, ensuring that there will be no progress. Categorizing an alcohol-fueled incident based on the location or context in which it occurs facilitates its dismissal as just another routine news event. This robs it of meaning and ensures an end to curiosity and understanding.

Contexts are important. Law enforcement knows well the danger of walking into the emotional turmoil of domestic disputes. It's the most dangerous call for a police officer, even if alcohol is not involved. Contexts combine with all of the contributing factors to structure the probability of the consequences that might follow. Separating cause from both context and consequence is a step toward clarity and improved understanding.

Life is full of frustrations, insecurities, failures, and success. Hard times and easy times are all part of the mix. These normal ups and downs may lead to drinking as an escape and the pathologies that follow, including hostility. But the context of life is not the cause of the aggression. An attempt to explain behavior by pointing to the context in which it occurs contributes to the confusion and perpetuates lack of awareness of what is actually happening.

This is why we need the new perspective on alcohol and aggression that HRA and the neuroscience of inflammation give us. If there is any hope of increasing public awareness, we need a framework that facilitates understanding of this ongoing personal and social problem.

Disrupting an airplane in midair puts the importance of cause, context, and consequence in a neat bundle of indisputable reality. The closed quarters of an airplane sharply clarifies HRA. All onboard are vulnerable, perched in midair, forcing attention when a passenger is drunk and hostile. It's a closed laboratory for HRA.

On a flight from Atlanta to Orange County, California a 43-year-old man, flying with his mother and girlfriend, demonstrated how too many shots of hard liquor can lead to belligerence. He says he blacked out, but his belligerence and disruptive behavior resulted in the plane being diverted to Albuquerque. "He allegedly threw trash and bottles into the aisles of the airplane and was loud and disruptive." [43]

This fellow had four shots of liquor before boarding and the staff served him another four on the plane. The authorities declined to press charges. It's true that some people don't become belligerent after drinking, but I wonder if given enough liquor and time, whether all of us are susceptible to the brain inflammation, hostility, and blackouts that alcohol causes.

With a drunk, there is always something that precedes the eruption of anger—and when anger gains momentum, escalation happens fast. On a flight from New York to Phoenix, a 39-year-old woman became upset over the rules concerning use of the restroom. The conflict started when she was told to wait because it was occupied. This seems like a reasonable rule, but it didn't go over well with her. The woman became angry. The flight attendant testified at the court hearing that she didn't know why the woman became angry.

After using the restroom, she took her seat and watched the flight attendant enter the cockpit, at which point she went up to the door and began banging on it. The co-pilot came out and the woman screamed at him and hit him four times. He went back in the cabin while the ranting and raving continued. The woman began harassing passengers, telling them that she worked for the Mayor of New York and could get them arrested.

One paragraph stood out in this article:

"The cause is under dispute, but FBI Supervisory Special Agent...said 'the investigation indicates alcohol abuse played a significant role in the incident.'" [44]

That's as close as it gets to singling out alcohol in an official statement. Now we can go just a little further: She became angry due to brain inflammation caused by alcohol.

In another case, a 49-year-old female attorney on a red eye flight from Perth to Brisbane, Australia started shouting obscenities and flailing her arms when she was refused more alcohol.

As the story unfolded, it seems that she was drunk when she got on the plane and then had a few more drinks before the staff realized she was in trouble. Many air-rage drunks start drinking before boarding and are sent over the edge of civil behavior by just a few more after they board. In the words of this passenger, it was the last two bourbons that made her drunk.

She was fined after her arrest and had a few interesting comments about responsibility: "The fine was ridiculous because, after all, the airline did serve me alcohol. The airline is responsible for what they serve." [45] That statement is an interesting escape from personal responsibility. It almost sounds as if she were still drunk.

The feeling of entitlement to more alcohol is often the starting point of an argument that can easily escalate to major airline-passenger inconvenience. Free drink coupons due to a delayed takeoff caused a flight to Las Vegas to make an unscheduled landing to remove 16 people.

According to the FBI agent in charge, some were angry and abusive because they felt the free-drink coupons should be worth more than one drink. Others were upset because the staff refused to serve them because they were too drunk. Most of them ended up cuffed and marching through the airport; some were not only because the police ran out of cuffs. One of the officers noted that it was unlikely they had ever been handcuffed before.

Federal charges of interfering with a flight were brought against one of the passengers, who threw a beer can and a cup of ice at his favorite flight attendant.

The pilot diverted to the nearest airport because the crew felt their safety was at risk. It sounds as if there was a riot building. Most of those removed were middle-aged or older, not young people. The one that was sure to face federal charges was 32. Some of the others may have been charged as well. What an inconvenience for all involved. This was not the easy and fun trip to Las Vegas they expected. The FBI agent supervising the arrest said: "I've been an agent for coming up on 25 years. I've never seen this many people involved in a crime-aboard-aircraft incident." [46]

Some of the 172 passengers did not react with hostility toward the crew, but 16 did and caused the plane to stop short of the Las Vegas destination. Should we conclude that the passengers who were not removed simply were not drunk enough to exhibit HRA?

This case makes me think more people are subject to HRA than we might think. Some have a high threshold and some have a low threshold. But all of us have a threshold. If we step across it, we enter the land of Hyde. Certainly, there were a number of contributing factors that singled out the group that was arrested. For example, sitting in close proximity to one particularly belligerent member is likely to ease the escalation of those nearby. It's one thing to feel irritated and angry. It's entirely different for momentum to build into a concert of hostile passengers, each feeding off the others with the courage of drunken indignation.

"Alcohol Is the Leading Cause"

Bangor, Maine is the airport for out-of-control passengers on U.S. flights, and sometimes international flights disrupted while crossing the Atlantic. The airport is a former Air Force base with a runway that is more than 11,000 feet long. That length makes for an easy landing under stressful situations. Here are two cases of British citizens landing drunk in Bangor.

In one case, a 25-year old Brit broke some video equipment and then moved on to smash an interior window of the plane while yelling that he hoped the passengers would "get sucked out and die." Of course, he would be the first out if it happened. As you might imagine, he had no memory of the incident, in classic blackout fashion. He got 60 days in jail and had to pay $28,875 in restitution.

In the second case, a 41-year old man from Manchester attacked two flight attendants who had refused to serve him more liquor. This conflict got bloody and the crew had to tie the man up with cloth napkins and sit on him until they landed in Bangor. The FBI agent in Bangor commented that the leading cause for unplanned landings in Bangor was alcohol. [48]

The cause of air rage is not the airplane in which the hostility erupts, any more than the cause of domestic violence is the house in which the fight occurs. The cause is a reaction to alcohol. The context is an airplane. The consequence is an appearance in court, which might be in a remote town in Maine.

Hostility reactions on airplanes are very focused. It is a confined space with no exit. And the aisle is lined with witnesses who have a personal interest in keeping enough order to land safely. Given the structured nature of this context, it is hard to miss an outburst of alcohol-fueled hostility.

Elliott Hester, a former flight attendant and author of *Plane Insanity*, a book concerning misbehavior in flight, says, "Most in-flight transgressions (can be) attributed to three factors: alcohol, liquor and booze." Hester goes on to say: "In my flying experience (and based on research I've done for many articles) the majority of violent/abusive in-flight incidents are a result of drunkenness." [49]

Drunk passengers on Russian flights led to the consideration of banning alcohol on flights. Drunk when they got on the plane and drinking more while in flight, these passengers caused an interior minister official to state: "I don't rule out that we will raise the question of the need to prohibit alcoholic drinks aboard airplanes." His statement followed a 10-hour delay because a handful of drunk passengers became confrontational with the crew and were smoking on the plane. [50]

"Alcohol Was Definitely a Factor"

The complete insanity of some people who get drunk and hostile illustrates the extremes that comprise the spectrum of behaviors we see as HRA.

The behavior of some people would better be described as psychotic, and might be if they weren't drunk. But after centuries of witnessing these extremes, we humans tend to dismiss crazed reactions to alcohol as simple drunkenness. The craziness is part of human behavior and one more method we use to hurt each other. Defining drunken rage as HRA is a step toward clarity. Recognizing HRA as inflammation of the brain is a step toward acknowledging the neurological cause of the insanity behind the reaction, and perhaps a step toward public awareness.

A flight to Hong Kong made an unscheduled landing in Anchorage after a drunk passenger started screaming obscenities and ended by tearing a phone off the wall and fighting with flight attendants. It took a crew member and four passengers to bring him down and get the cuffs on. Of course, there was a build-up escalating to the ultimate blow-up. It started with a demand for free drinks and criticism of the attendant when she refused.

The disrupter had about five drinks. The FBI agent in charge said "alcohol was definitely a factor." [52]

In August of 2013, a flight from New York to Shanghai was diverted to Anchorage. A woman in the fashion business had five glasses of wine plus whatever she could steal from the galley, according to passengers who saw the drama unfold. When the balance tipped to hostility, this 47-year-old walked the aisles cursing, and in case some passengers had missed the performance, climbed on the seats to make herself known. The crew went through the respectful motions of asking her to return to her seat and eventually issued a written notice that she had refused a safety order. She hit the attendant with the notice and demanded to be let off the plane.

Eventually, the pilot confronted her and asked if she would follow the instructions of the crew. She refused, and the plane headed for Anchorage to fulfill her wish to be let off the flight. Her two children, who were with her, went on to Shanghai to be met by their father. Can you believe that a middle-aged woman riding in first class would behave like this when she was responsible for her children on an airplane? When the police boarded to remove her, she was "physically combative." She ended up in jail and the plane continued on. [53]

With time and enough alcohol, all people who are intoxicated seem to have the potential to become belligerent. Time spent drinking, the amount consumed, and circumstance play important roles in determining who displays the ever-present potential for hostility. Drink a lot in a short time and the odds increase for HRA and a blackout.

HRA on airplanes captures both time and the quantity of alcohol consumed in a toxic mix that can't escape scrutiny. Drink to the point of hostility, and every person within earshot will know. These examples illustrate how people are unpredictably subject to HRA when a lot of alcohol is consumed in a short time period. Often, it is a surprise and an embarrassment for the people caught in the drama. They didn't expect to become belligerent or to be dressed in jail-house orange, sleeping it off on a hard bunk. What a surprise.

When airlines distribute free drink coupons, the last thing they imagine is that those gifts, designed to make customers happy, will increase the probability that the "happy" customers will become hostile toward the crew and passengers and precipitate an unscheduled landing at the nearest airport. To a large extent, we are dealing with probabilities: Drink a lot in a short period and the chances of HRA increase.

Start with an argument and an exchange of demands. Then move to physical hostility, and you have the simple, visible pattern of escalation typical of most drunken confrontations. Hidden in this process is the frequent blackout of memory and the not-so-hidden inability to reason. I asked a friend who volunteers at the local suicide prevention hotline if she ever had to talk with a drunk caller. Her answer reflected the practical nature of the work. She explained that they are trained not to talk to drunks because there is no chance of reasoning with them. This is an important perspective, founded on years of dealing with serious situations. Keep it in mind if you are caught in the frustration of trying to talk to a manipulative drinker.

Chapter Six

Crossing the Threshold to Hostility

"I'd Never Seen Anything Like It"

I was sitting in a crowded bar on a Friday after work along with about ten co-workers in a farewell tribute to one of us who was moving on. I was watching waiters carry trays with pitchers of beer to the side room, when I noticed four of them coming the other way with something alive. Each held a quarter of a person, writhing and yelling face up toward the ceiling and moving head first toward the exit. That was an obvious hostility reaction, requiring action worthy of an old-West saloon.

During this surprise performance, I was thinking that these waiters knew what they were doing and must have had a lot of practice. There was no way that fellow was going to escape. I saw a similar episode in Mexico City many years earlier. A friend and I were in an upscale downtown bar, having one of the fine Mexican beers, when I heard screaming and saw a man grabbing bottles of sauce from the table and trying to drink them. He was dressed in a suit, seemed well-to-do, but was lamenting his relationship with his mother or someone else's mother—my Spanish is hit and miss. This time, two unusually large men appeared out of the shadows.

Each took an arm and lifted the distraught person who was quite large also, and ushered him to the door. It seems the bartender had cut off his alcohol and so he moved on to the bottles of sauce on the table—too hot to drink for anyone sober.

Throwing people out of a bar has its dangers. They might come back. At one of the older establishments—now demolished—not far from where I live, two men were enjoying a beer and the best bar burritos ever made in the 1970s. They must have been getting a little loud and causing a distraction as the afternoon wore on. At some point, the owner arrived, noticed that one of the fellows had a machete strapped to his belt, and told him that he had to leave because no weapons were allowed in the bar. It went downhill from there. There was a fist fight and the usual screaming and yelling as the owner and staff threw them out.

When the rowdies returned they had shotguns plus the machete. What they didn't know was that the owner was a retired state trooper and knew how to handle himself around fist fights and guns. They exchanged many rounds. The bar itself served as a good barrier for bird shot and Mr. Machete was no match for the owner's service revolver. Of course, the owner wasn't drunk and was a trained marksman. It was a fog of a fight; when the smoke cleared, the two intruders were dispatched to their just reward.

By the time the police arrived, the mess had quieted for obvious reasons, but the owner was having chest pains. Sadly, the excitement was too much and he died on the spot of a heart attack—an unexpected consequence of a very intense bar fight.

Once the threshold between alcohol and hostility is crossed, it's prudent to expect trouble. Ejecting a patron from the bar is best followed with a wary eye to the door for a possible return. In one case, a woman was thrown out of a sports bar for fighting. The staff had refused to serve her, which is a trigger for drinker discontent. This young woman waited until closing time and returned to attack the staff, not with a shotgun, but with pepper spray. [54] It could have been worse. Just getting the belligerent out the door does not eliminate the hostility.

Someone I went to school with was in a bar and watched an altercation unfold. It was a knock-down drag-out fight, resulting in the instigator being pushed out the door. Deciding that this was not the kind of situation he wanted to be part of, he walked out. The trouble was that he didn't wait long enough. The belligerent was standing just outside the door, watching for the first teeth to walk through. A couple of my school mate's teeth ended up on the sidewalk, and the belligerent ran off. He didn't care who he hit — first out the door was good enough.

Sometimes the tables are turned and the drunk belligerent gets a surprise. A friend of mine who has studied judo since childhood was walking in the parking lot toward the entrance to his favorite bar when a fellow who had just been ejected came toward him. He had fight written all over his face as he reached toward my friend. His expression probably changed as he flew through the air and landed solidly on the pavement, ending any chance of continued combat.

Many years ago, there was a visiting student from Japan at UNM. He was bowling with other students one night when a bowler in a different group who had consumed too many beers started harassing him. They moved the escalating altercation outside. As one witness described the scene to me, "The drunk got as sick as anyone I have ever seen." All it took was one accurate punch to the solar plexus and the drunk began disgorging the evening's beer and more. What the drunk had no way of knowing was that our guest student was an experienced street fighter with plenty of practice from the riots in Tokyo.

Bar fights are a normal part of drinking life. Bartenders are always on the lookout for troublemakers and can become skilled at defusing tense situations. The vast majority of bar patrons expect to have a good time without threat of violence. It doesn't always work out that way. Some are transformed into the Hyde personality by alcohol, and it's likely that, within some circles, individuals get liquored up first and go looking for trouble. Either way, alcohol is behind the hostile intent.

A friend told me about her experience when she was out one night during college. One member of the group was known to react aggressively to alcohol, and the other men had learned to head off trouble before it got out of hand.

They were standing in a crowded bar drinking for about an hour, talking, when she turned and saw a different person. This young man had changed from a friendly, kind, and thoughtful person to Hyde in the blink of an eye. She told me "I'd never seen anything like it." His face was red and swollen, and his eyes were narrow, dark holes. He started elbowing and shoving people, and that's when his friends stepped in and got him out of the bar. It didn't escalate beyond that, but his facial expression left a lasting impression. "I truly have never seen anything like it. He didn't look like the same person. I wouldn't have recognized him if I hadn't been standing there."

This was a one-time experience of the face of Hyde, and she knew instantly something was wrong. We have an inherent ability to recognize faces and changes in expression that form the first indication of emotion, both good and bad. In this case, the change was so stark and occurred in such a relatively short time that the incident stood out in her memory, and remains something she will probably never forget. Furthermore, her description reflects several elements of the inflammatory effects of alcohol. The swollen area around the eyes, the red face, and hostile aggression all point to widespread inflammation and the body's reaction to the toxic effects of alcohol.

I remember one fellow who was predictably susceptible to HRA. He was a teacher who spent the summers working as a logger out of a small town in Idaho where I worked for the Forest Service during college. He was well known to the local sheriff, who would break up his altercations by saying, "I told you if you want to beat up someone you have to take them down the hill to the next county." This seemed to work most of the time. The morning after one contentious confrontation, a friend of mine had coffee with this fellow and was impressed with what a nice guy he was. It was only when he drank that he went looking for trouble.

During this conversation, he apologized for his behavior and said he didn't know why he got this way when he drank. Exactly how did he behave? Basically, he threw his weight around the bar and if someone brushed against him in the process, it was an immediate grab to the front of the shirt with the question, "Why did you

93

bump into me?" He combined the courage of impaired reason with the hostility that precedes serious physical confrontation. He was a dangerous bully who went looking for a fight, but only after a couple of beers. Otherwise, he was a nice guy who likely will be remembered only as a mean drunk.

One of the recurring themes of HRA is the puzzle for the day-after sober drunk when he tries to understand what possessed him during the hostile episode. Blackouts are not the issue in these cases. There is a sense of wonder that possesses thinking, educated individuals who struggle to explain their own hostile behavior that makes a blackout seem simple.

"I Still Wonder How It Happened"

Most of the insight concerning HRA is found in the statements of the hostiles themselves. Even in the sunshine of sober reality, the fog of drunken violence is difficult to penetrate. But when a drunk is sober and looking back on his actions with puzzlement, it illuminates this mystery like nothing else can.

Knowing what goes on in the brain when alcohol unleashes chaos can go a long way to helping the victims get through the aftermath. Alcohol causes inflammation. The hostile reaction that so many experience is part of the inflammation process acting on the aggression centers of the brain. If you are caught in the web of alcohol and hostility and wonder what is happening, perhaps viewing it as an inflammation process will help your understanding.

In one especially difficult case, a judge said that both defendants were law abiding until the night they attacked and slashed the faces of two bartenders. This case was particularly difficult because the aftermath resulted in the suicide of one of the bartenders because of his disfigured face.

All of the participants were in their late twenties. One of the attackers held two jobs, both were educated, and neither had a history of trouble with the law. One attorney did say that his client was intoxicated and showed bad judgment. His client appealed to the judge during sentencing, saying: "I understand what I did was wrong ... I did something out of stupidity and drunkenness ... I still wonder how it happened and why it happened. I am sorry." [55]

Struggling to find an answer is a good first step toward insight. This young, suffering survivor was thinking, not dismissing his attack as acceptable and expected drunken behavior. He was asking what happened to him and why it happened. The danger is that we have gotten used to this type of drunken behavior and have given up on finding an answer. It doesn't have to be that way.

"I'm Not Sure How Things Can Get Much Worse"

Is it possible that a drinking culture can get so far out of control that it overwhelms the police? Bar fights that spill into the streets and continue with escalating violence outside of clubs and pubs throughout Britain describe the scene facing a former Boston police chief when he was hired by the U.K. to reduce the crime rate.

His first move was to consider "new proposals from senior police officers for tough new sanctions against violent drinkers." This was one situation in which it was unavoidably clear that binge drinking was causing the chaos. The U.K. made the Wild West of the U.S. look like child's play. It required action. Among the proposals were: "binge drinkers caught fighting in city centres" would be given points on their driver's licenses; fighters would be banned from bars with high crime; and "on-the-spot penalty fines, sting operations on businesses serving under-age drinkers, and closure notices on pubs and clubs associated with violence."

After observing the situation, this American 'super-cop' summed up his assessment and his approach:

"If you're in the business of fighting crime, then you have to be in the business of dealing with the alcohol issue. I have spent an awful lot of Fridays and Saturday nights out here. At one or two o'clock in the morning these places are chaos. I'm not sure it can get much worse."

Weekends were the time for binge drinking, and the hospital records reflected the consequences: 70 percent of weekend hospital admissions were alcohol related. [57] It sounds like the drinking culture of the U.K. had turned the country into a boxing ring.

Binge drinking is the clue. Here is a clear indication that anyone who drinks a large amount of alcohol in a short time period increases the likelihood of having HRA. Not all people exhibit the reaction at the same time, but the probability of HRA increases when the amount consumed is large and the time in which it is consumed is brief.

We are dealing with probabilities when it comes to HRA. Some people are more at risk and have a higher probability of reacting with hostility than others. Certainty has no place when it comes to human behavior. That's why we impose models on observed reality that help interpret the meaning of behavior.

For example, here we are using the model of cause, context, and consequence to frame the spectrum of behaviors we call HRA. This model is an aid to help us break out of old ways of thinking that are no longer useful.

The British experience of binge drinking is a good example of conflict confined in time — weekends. It focuses on hostility in a defined time period, with no doubt of the alcohol-causal relationship, in part because of the context of pubs and clubs spilling into street violence. The consequence is also easy to see in the police reaction and weekend hospital admissions. Cause, context, and consequence help us frame this behavior to better understand it.

This same model works well for other expressions of HRA, such as domestic violence and air rage. Understanding human behavior is a challenge that can be overcome when you frame what you observe in a way that allows meaningful interpretation.

Domestic violence, air rage, and bar fights — with a high degree of likelihood — share the same HRA cause. The contexts vary, which can sometimes obscure the cause. The consequences also vary and can carry great emotion for all, thus tending to cloud meaningful interpretation. A model that uses all three areas to frame events is useful because it helps separate reason from emotion, broadens understanding, and guards against narrowing our view to the point of missing real meaning.

"From One Fight to Another"
Street brawls flowing out of bars are not exclusive to Britain. In Key West, Florida, the party atmosphere can extend well into the early hours because the bars don't

close until four in the morning. This causes serious problems for the police.

A sergeant was picked up and slammed to the ground by a tourist outside of a bar. He responded with his baton. Complaints were filed against the officer. There are dozens of bars on the main street, with enough tourists and alcohol to fuel real trouble. As the police chief said, "Early in the morning on Duval Street, my guys sometimes go from one fight to another. There's too much alcohol and too many people in one small area." [58]

The street fights of Britain and Key West seem to be bordering on mob riots. Anyone who follows spring break activity knows groups can get to the point of riot fast and can understand why any police force would be jumpy.

I remember being locked in a bar in Coeur d'Alene, Idaho after the owner noticed the police moving in to disperse a crowd of drunk students with tear gas. Clearly, the bar owner had prior years of experience with visiting student celebrations. My friend and I were lucky that we were in the bar at the time, not on the street. After an hour or so, when things had quieted, the owner unlocked the doors. As we walked from the refuge into the residual tear gas, I learned why the name "tear gas" is so very perfect and works so well.

Drunken mobs in bars are an order of magnitude more dangerous than two-party fights, especially when they target a lone individual. In Manila, a drunk sailor made the mistake of singing a popular song out of tune. Ten drunks in the audience took offence, jeering him. They waited outside the bar and attacked him and his two friends as they left. The singer died of stab wounds, and his two friends survived with a beating. [59]

It seems that many of the arguments that start in bars become physical confrontations outside, often involving several ganging up on one with unimaginable and horrible consequences. These extreme examples, although difficult to read about, remove any doubt that the brain inflammation caused by alcohol is a serious problem. If you like horror films, some of the real-life stories you have read here may seem mild. However, many of the participants here don't get to stand up and wash off fake blood and get on with their lives. These stories are the end.

Heavy rocks to the head are a frequent termination tool. A bar fight in a now-closed bar in Albuquerque started inside and moved out to the parking lot where a row of 98-pound boulders formed a barrier around the club. A more aware design would never have provided such handy weapons. Perhaps 98 pounds seemed immovable or there was denial that a fight would ever result in such a heavy object being dropped on a head. That's exactly what happened, after the victim had been beaten unconscious by the attacker and his friends. [60]

There's momentum to any aggressive act. Sometimes it can't stop until irreparable damage is complete. This is true with verbal attacks as well as physical fights. The difference is that verbal attacks in the extreme continue until the relationship is terminated — not the life.

Chapter Seven

It's Madness

When you accept that alcohol causes hostile aggression, the next step is to figure out what happens in the brain that produces hostile behavior. Ultimately, we look to science to clarify the mechanism that triggers HRA. Cytokines acting on the aggression centers of the brain are the most likely candidates. This is a new direction in alcohol-pathology research and a first step toward the eventual clarification of the exact mechanisms involved.

HRA is caused by inflammation of the aggression centers of the brain after drinking alcohol. This is not the ordinary inflammation you think of, consisting of redness and swelling around a cut. Inflammation in this sense is the action of proinflammatory cytokines overwhelming anti-inflammatory cytokines as part of the immune system's response to the threat of alcohol.

Aggression and hostility in this case can be interpreted as a product of the cytokine activity in the brain attempting to protect the individual. Misguided and counterproductive best describe the activity of this cytokine disruption. We see HRA as the outcome, in the form of domestic violence, air rage, bar fights, and in many other contexts. The social and personal consequences are destructive, costly and, in human relations, life altering.

The spectrum of behaviors that comprise HRA are often difficult to connect to alcohol, especially the less extreme verbal variety. Making the connection requires that you know a connection is there to be made. The challenge is to see what is happening, as it is happening in the midst of chaotic emotions.

A damaged life for everyone involved is the usual outcome of binge and chronic drinking and the resulting HRA. Damage can be repaired, and drinking problems can be controlled. Knowledge is power—the power to take control. Knowing the cause can bring clarity. Seeing HRA in context brings insight. Understanding the consequences brings self-reliant action. Individual choice remains primary; without it, nothing can be accomplished.

All the drama and hostility surrounding alcohol is madness in the old sense of the word. "Mad" captures the meaning of being both angry and insane. A person who had gone mad in times gone by would be referred to today as "insane" or "psychotic." The behavior characteristic of HRA can be considered a low-level form of temporary madness. It is an antisocial reaction stemming from the traditional social activity of drinking. Hostility is such a deviation from expected social drinking behavior that it's understandable why acknowledging the problem meets resistance.

HRA is expressed in a broad spectrum of emotions and behaviors described in the examples throughout this book. These terms and others describe a mean drunk.

Irritable
Angry
Hostile
Controlling
Demanding

Labeling
Blaming
Belittling
Demeaning
Criticizing
Arguing
Fighting

The following are examples of hostility that can appear in the interaction between the mean drunk and the target.

A mother complaining to her daughter about how she chooses to live.

A father complaining to his son about his failures in life.

A wife complaining to her husband.

A young couple arguing every night.

A husband beating his wife.

Two young men in a fist fight.

A woman attacking a bartender.

A passenger attacking an airline attendant.

A friend stabbing a friend.

Friends crushing the skull of a friend.

It's very easy to discount alcohol as a cause for the everyday hostility you might experience from a family member, especially if it's only verbal. Stop for a minute and consider the possibility that alcohol is the root cause, and that the pain you are experiencing is the product of the drinker's brain inflammation.

Memories are fallible and short; consequently, for the evidence to have impact, it is best viewed as cumulative and seen as a pattern over time. To accomplish this requires reviewing incidents of hostile behavior and an ability to interpret meaningful patterns. That process is the only way, short of extensive personal experience, to understand the pervasiveness of HRA. Adding to the difficulty of accumulating evidence is that the hostility reaction is not consistent or predictable from individual to individual—although you might take issue with that statement if you live with a heavy drinker.

Nevertheless, inconsistent hostility tends to promote disagreement. If you grew up in a heavy-drinking family riddled with argument and worse, you might have trouble convincing a peer who grew up in a more stable environment that HRA was even real. Experience is the best teacher, and when it comes to the ravages of alcohol, there is no substitute. Hard science may be the one exception.

We look to hard science to validate what we observe in real life. Science has the potential of proof and the promise of final understanding that makes sense out of the chaos. We have made a first step by discovering that cytokines elicit a rage response when microinjected into the areas of the brain associated with aggression. [24]

We have simplified this complex process by describing it as brain inflammation. Gene expression, serotonin receptors, the location of the cytokine attack, the inhibitory strength of anti-inflammatory cytokines, and GABAA receptors all play roles. Complexity of this sort accounts for the variation in immediacy and intensity among individuals and probably is a clue as to why some people never exhibit hostility when drinking.

Cellular communication and activation by cytokines are the keys to understanding how alcohol triggers hostility.

Brain Inflammation

Threats come in many forms. The body, including the brain, responds, in part, to threats through the immune system. For example, the redness and swelling of inflammation around a cut is from cells that have been signaled by cytokines to isolate bacteria so it won't spread and infect more of the body. That is the helpful function of cytokines—as messengers signaling cells to take defensive action as part of the innate immune system. They are produced automatically in response to threats, but they can get out of hand.

The flu pandemic of 1918 was devastating because cytokine storms overwhelmed the bodies of those with strong immune systems. That is what killed so many healthy young adults—the body's attempt to fight the virus. The cytokine fight against alcohol is also out of hand in our society, taking over the brain and doing damage to relationships and endangering us in more ways than we can imagine. [36]

Perhaps understanding the neuromechanism involved will result in compassion toward the mean drunk just as compassion was found for the victims of the cytokine storms during the flu pandemic. Mean drunks are suffering-surviving victims no less than the targets of their hostility. It may be difficult to reach forgiveness if you are a target, but anyone can gain understanding and perhaps, compassion.

Sometimes we can reach the point of understanding only with great effort. The story of alcohol as reflected in *The Strange Case of Dr. Jekyll and Mr. Hyde* and well known in the literature of heavy drinking has not been recognized totally where it counts—scientifically. It seems we can never be sure of what we know in daily experience unless some objective scientific process confirms reality. But what a messy and frustrating process it can be, waiting for science to validate empirical observation and the validation to enter popular culture.

We are linking cytokines to hostility and then linking alcohol to cytokines in a causal chain by reviewing studies involving cytokines that elicit defensive aggression without alcohol, and then looking at studies that demonstrate that alcohol produces cytokines. Alcohol increases production of cytokines. Cytokines elicit hostility from the brain areas associated with aggression.

"Clinical reports describe increasing levels of hostility, anger, and irritability in patients who receive cytokine immunotherapy, and there are reports of a positive correlation between cytokine levels and aggressive behavior in non-patient populations." [24]

"Cytokines affect the brain and likely contribute to changes in the central nervous system that contribute to long-term changes in behavior and neurodegeneration. Together these studies suggest that ethanol disruption of cytokines and inflammation contribute in multiple ways to a diversity of alcoholic pathologies." [25]

The interaction of cytokines and inflammation and alcohol (ethanol) was clarified by a 2012 report by Liya Qin and Fulton T. Crews in the *Journal of Neuroinflammation*, which stated in part: "Increasing evidence links systemic inflammation to neuroinflammation and neurodegeneration." Importantly they conclude: "These studies indicate that TLR3 agonists increase blood cytokines that contribute to neurodegeneration and that ethanol binge drinking potentiates these responses." [26]

A 2007 review by Allan Siegel et al. details the complex interaction of neurotransmitters and brain regions and the limits of current understanding. The report ends with a reference to cytokines:

"An emerging path of investigation, based mainly on animal studies involving the use of cytokines for the regulation of aggression and rage behavior, is lacking in studies conducted along these lines in humans. Further investigations in this area conducted both on the animal and human level may hopefully reveal new insights into the mechanisms underlying aggression and rage behavior." [27]

The relationship between cytokines and alcohol is a subject of interest for researchers. In a 2010 study, circulating cytokines were found to be a possible biomarker of alcohol abuse:

"This is an emerging and potentially exciting avenue of research in that circulating cytokines may contribute to diagnostic biomarker panels and a combination of multiple biomarkers may significantly increase the sensitivity and specificity of the biochemical tests aiding reliable and accurate detection of excessive alcohol intake."[28]

To summarize, cytokines used in immunotherapy produced a noticeable change in mood in patients: hostility, anger, and irritability increased and became the subject of reports and further investigation. Certain cytokines applied to areas of the brain associated with aggression in cats stimulated defensive rage responses. [24] Separate and unrelated studies involving alcohol found that "disruption of cytokines and inflammation contribute in multiple ways to a diversity of alcoholic pathologies." [25] The relationship between alcohol and cytokines is strong enough that cytokines may prove useful as a biomarker of excessive alcohol intake. [28]

These studies present a chain of evidence that leads to the biomolecule that so far is the best candidate for the cause of HRA. Differences in the expression of individual genes, neurotransmitters, and cytokine reaction, and the amount and type of alcohol consumed over time, probably account for variations in the hostility reaction among individuals. This is not surprising because individuals are different in so many ways. With the understanding that there is always more to discover within the brain, for now we can say cytokines cause HRA.

It's normal for steps forward to be met with skepticism and doubt, as scientific dogmas and old models that express past understanding die off with time, and new proof replaces old belief. It took decades to complete a sufficient number of psychological studies to satisfy the requirements of the scientific method and finally verify that alcohol causes aggression. (Bushman, 1990) [10]

It took another 20 years for a comprehensive review of the neurobiological mechanisms of alcohol-related aggression to bring a broad picture of the issue into the arena of hard science. (Heinz et. al., 2011) [11] This slow scientific progress was underway even though the American Psychiatric Association had characterized and described intoxication using the language of aggression and fighting since at least 1980. [5]

Proving what we see in daily life takes time, research money, scientific curiosity, and new techniques of measurement. Science is a construction project, using the building blocks of past knowledge to complete a framework of understanding about how the world works. It is a big project that takes time.

Now we are moving to the challenges of the relatively difficult-to-measure area of neuroscience to further understand the neurobiological cause of what we have defined as HRA. The link between alcohol and hostility is the cytokine complex, which may eventually prove to involve the even smaller member of the cytokine family known as chemokines.

The cytokine-chemokine family has been measured in clusters and is associated with hostility even when immunotherapy is not involved. In a 2008 study of Dutch military men about to be deployed, hostility was found to be related to clusters of T-cell cytokines and chemokines:

"Hostility was significantly related to decreased IL-6/chemokine secretion and increased pro- and anti-inflammatory cytokines." [29]

Cytokines are signaling agents that warn cells of danger. They engage genes and neurotransmitters to take action. In the aggression centers of the brain, that action can result in hostility without the control of reason.

"Chronic inflammation is commonly associated with alcohol-related medical conditions. Accumulating evidence suggests that it acts as an etiological factor in the initiation and progression of many of these conditions. A significant number of illnesses of individuals with alcoholic liver diseases can be explained readily by a high level of circulating proinflammatory cytokines. Humans with variants of pro- and anti-inflammatory cytokine genes show increased susceptibility to alcoholic liver disease." [60]

Variations in pro- and anti-inflammatory cytokines and gene expression likely determine whether a person is a mean or happy drunk. Either reaction is incident based, not a permanent condition. When you realize where you fall in the range of behaviors, your responsibility to choose increases.

Balance is at the heart of health in so many cases. A balanced diet is the basis of proper nutrition. Moderation is essential to balance, if not the definition of balance itself. Balance between proinflammatory and anti-inflammatory cytokines makes for a healthy individual.

To throw the balance out of kilter is asking for trouble. This is the biological reason to drink with moderation, or not drink at all. If you drink to the point of hostility, you choose to surrender to a biological reaction. You surrender your free will and your individuality to the cytokine imbalance caused by alcohol. If you know you are a mean drunk and choose to drink anyway, remember that your responsibility to control your drinking is heavy. The damage you do to yourself and others is on you. You are solely accountable. You are free to choose.

Any attempt to understand the activity of the brain is an invitation to oversimplify. Neuroscience is a maze of specialized knowledge, with connections that give real meaning to the frustrations in the story of the Tower of Babel. Connecting the biology of the brain with the behavior of humans adds to the challenge. Advances in neuroscience will modify current knowledge by clarifying or completely changing current understanding. But for now, all we need is sufficient understanding of the neurobiology of HRA to improve our approach to the personal and social problems it causes.

Mean Drunk started as an attempt to solve a puzzle that has haunted me for most of my life. I knew that the cause of HRA had to be an active change in the brain and not the result of disinhibition, which was so popular in the literature in the past. If disinhibition causes alcohol-related hostility, the implication is that humans are innately cruel. I have always thought humans—for the most part— were innately kind, flawed, and prone to folly, but not programmed for cruelty. This conviction kept my search going for the active neurobiological cause, as I confronted conventional wisdom.

There are so many examples of HRA and the damage it causes that my challenge became how to tell the story without overwhelming the reader. Before I found the connection between hostility, cytokines, and alcohol, I thought *Mean Drunk* might be nothing more than a pile of empirical observations, creating a massive statement of the obvious with no causal answer. Thankfully for all involved, the immune system came to the rescue and I was able to isolate cytokines as a likely candidate for the neurobiological cause of HRA. This is in no way the final answer. It's a basis for further research to find a complete explanation of the mechanisms involved. The immune system we humans live with is powerful. It affects our mental and physical health while holding exciting promise for our self-understanding. [61]

One of the reasons I wrote *Mean Drunk* was to explain how a person who loves you can treat you so poorly. The explanation is HRA—a neurobiological reaction to alcohol. If you have been or are a target of HRA, I hope this book will help you cope.

I'm convinced that when you understand a problem you increase your ability to adapt—your awareness is sharper and your choices expand. Just making the effort to figure out a problem is a step toward independent, critical thinking. This allows you to move toward a life of self-reliance based on informed choice.

114

Notes

1. *Pueblo Men Say Beer, Fight Led To Death*, Scott Sandlin, Albuquerque Journal September 8, 1990 E, 2.

2. Robert Louis Stevenson (1886) *The Strange Case of Dr. Jekyll and Mr. Hyde*.

3. *Alcoholics Anonymous*, The Big Book, Third Edition, New York: 1976, p. 21.

4. *Johnny Carson's Darker Side*, November 24, 2004, ET Newslink via Yahoo! Entertainment.
"Johnny Carson will forever be a man remembered for bringing laughter to TV audiences everywhere, but ET recently uncovered an interview that shows a very different and darker side of the legend. In a 1979 *60 Minutes* profile with Mike Wallace, the famous NBC host of *The Tonight Show* opened up about his drinking and smoking. 'I just found out I do not drink well,' he confessed to Wallace. 'When I did drink, rather that a lot of people who become fun loving and gregarious and love everybody — I would go to the opposite.'"

5. *American Psychiatric Association: Diagnostic and Statistical Manual of Mental Disorders*, Third Edition Washington, D.C. APA: 1980 p. 132 (Commonly referred to as DSM-III).

6. DSM-III (1980) p. 131.

7. DSM-III-R (1987) p. 128.

8. DSM-IV (1994) p. 197.

9. Aaron M. White (2004) *What Happened? Alcohol, Memory Blackouts, and the Brain*, National Institute on Alcohol Abuse and Alcoholism.

"Alcohol primarily interferes with the ability to form new long-term memories, leaving intact previously established long-term memories and the ability to keep new information active in memory for brief periods. As the amount of alcohol consumed increases, so does the magnitude of the memory impairments. Large amounts of alcohol, particularly if consumed rapidly, can produce partial (i.e., fragmentary) or complete (i.e., en bloc) blackouts, which are periods of memory loss for events that transpired while a person was drinking. Blackouts are much more common among social drinkers — including college drinkers — than was previously assumed, and have been found to encompass events ranging from conversations to intercourse. Mechanisms underlying alcohol-induced memory impairments include disruption of activity in the hippocampus, a brain region that plays a central role in the formation of new autobiographical memories."

10. Bushman, B. J. and Cooper, H. M. Effects of Alcohol on Human Aggression: An Integrative Research Review. *Psychological Bulletin* 1990 Vol. 107, No. 3, 341-354.

"This review used quantitative and qualitative techniques to integrate the alcohol and aggression literature. The primary purpose of the review was to determine if a causal relation exists between alcohol and aggression. The main meta-analysis included 30 experimental studies that used between-subjects designs, male confederate, and male subjects who were social drinkers. Studies using other designs or subject populations were integrated with meta-analytic procedures when possible and summarized descriptively when not. The results of the review indicate that alcohol does indeed cause aggression. However, alcohol effects were moderated by certain methodological parameters."

"Correlational evidence, however, does not allow one to infer that alcohol is the cause of violent crime (e.g., Brain, 1986). Experimental data must be used to make such inferences. Thus, the present review includes only studies that used the experimental method to examine the relation between alcohol and aggression."

11. Heinz A.J., Beck, Meyer-Lindenberg, Sterzer, and Heinz A. Cognitive and neurobiological mechanisms of alcohol-related aggression, *Nature Reviews Neuroscience* 2011 June 2; 12 (7): 400-13.

"Alcohol-related violence is a serious and common social problem. Moreover, violent behaviour is much more common in alcohol-dependent individuals. Animal experiments and human studies have provided insights into the acute effect of alcohol on aggressive behaviour and into common factors underlying acute and chronic alcohol intake and aggression. These studies have shown that environmental factors, such as early-life stress, interact with genetic variations in serotonin-related genes that affect serotonergic and GABAergic neurotransmission. This leads to increased alcohol intake and impulsive aggression. In addition, acute and chronic alcohol intake can further impair executive control and thereby facilitate aggressive behaviour."

12. Susan Montoya Bryan, *Justice Reform Slow in Indian Country*, The Associated Press via the Albuquerque Journal January 27, 2013, B, 1.

"Scenes like this are far too common in Indian Country, where violent crime rates on some reservations are 20 times the national average. Women are especially vulnerable; federal statistics show that nearly half of all American Indian and Alaska Native women have experienced physical violence, sexual assault or stalking by an intimate partner and that 1 in 3 will be raped."

13. *O, The Oprah Magazine*, February, 2013.

14. Jeremy Pawloski, *Man Accused in Attack on Mother.* Albuquerque Journal, November 20, 2004, E, 2.

15. Robert Rodriguez, *Son Held in Mother's Death After Beating*, Albuquerque Journal, September 24, 1992, A, 1.

16. Jeff Proctor, *APD Internal Affairs targets 4 supervisors, Group was at bar before sergeant's alleged attack on wife*, Albuquerque Journal February 19, 2013, A, 1.

17. Susan Shultz and David DesRouches, *CBS news anchor arrested for choking wife in Darien*, Darien Times, February 18, 2013.

18. Gerri Hirshey, *My Lifelong Teammate – My Mother*, Parade, February 1, 2004.

19. Samuel Maull, *Judge Tosses Assault Suit*, The Associated Press via the Albuquerque Journal September 26, 2006, A, 6.

20. T.J. Wilham, *Cops Put Decades-Old Case to Rest*, Albuquerque Journal, August 25, 2006 A, 1.

21. *Why They Beat the Odds*, The Oprah Winfrey Show March 1, 2007.

22. DSM-III (1980) p. 129.

23. *Jealousy Motive Suspected in Death*, Albuquerque Journal, October 24, 2003, B, 2.

24. Steven S. Zalcman and Allan Siegel, The neurobiology of aggression and rage: role of cytokines. *Brain, Behavior, and Immunity* 2006 Nov; 20 (6): 507-14.
"Recent studies have suggested an important relationship linking cytokines, immunity and aggressive behavior. Clinical reports describe increasing levels of hostility, anger, and irritability in patients who receive cytokine immunotherapy, and there are reports of a positive correlation between cytokine levels and aggressive behavior in non-patient populations. On the basis of these reports and others describing the presence or actions of different cytokines in regions of the brain associated with aggressive behavior, our laboratory embarked upon a program of research designed to identify and characterize the role of IL-1 and IL-2 in the hypothalamus and midbrain periaqueductal gray (PAG)—two regions functionally linked through reciprocal anatomical connections—in the regulation of feline defensive rage. A paradigm involved cytokine

microinjections into either medial hypothalamus and elicitation of defensive rage behavior from the PAG or vice versa. These studies have revealed that both cytokines have potent effects in modulating defensive rage behavior. With respect to IL-1, this cytokine facilitates defensive rage when microinjected into either the medial hypothalamus or PAG and these potentiating effects are mediated through 5-HT2 receptors. In contrast, the effects of IL-2 are dependent upon the anatomical locus. IL-2 microinjected into the medial hypothalamus suppresses defensive rage and this suppression is mediated through GABAA receptors, while microinjections of IL-2 in the PAG potentiate defensive rage, in which these effects are mediated through NK-1 receptors. Present research is designed to further delineate the roles of cytokines in aggressive behavior and to begin to unravel the possible signaling pathways involved in this process."

25. Crews FT, Bechara R, Brown LA, Guidot DM, Mandrekar P, Oak S, Qin L, Szabo G, Wheeler M, Zou J., Cytokines and alcohol. *Alcoholism: Clinical Experimental Research* 2006 Apr; 30 (4); 720-30.

"Cytokines are multifunctional proteins that play a critical role in cellular communication and activation. Cytokines have been classified as being proinflammatory (T helper 1, Th1) or anti-inflammatory (T helper 2, Th2) depending on their effects on the immune system. However, cytokines impact a variety of tissues including plasma, lung, liver, and brain. Studies on human monocyte responses to pathogens reveal ethanol disruption of cytokine production depending upon the pathogen and duration of alcohol consumption, with multiple pathogens and chronic ethanol promoting inflammatory cytokine production. In lung, cytokine production is disrupted by ethanol exacerbating respiratory distress syndrome with greatly increased expression of transforming growth factor beta (TGFbeta). Alcoholic liver disease involves an inflammatory hepatitis and an exaggerated Th1 response with increases in tumor necrosis factor alpha (TNFalpha). Recent studies suggest that the transition from Th1 to Th2 cytokines contribute to hepatic fibrosis and cirrhosis. Cytokines affect the brain and likely contribute to changes in the central nervous system that contribute to long-term changes in behavior and neurodegeneration. Together these studies suggest that ethanol disruption of cytokines and inflammation contribute in multiple ways to a diversity of alcoholic pathologies."

26. Qui L. and Crews F. T., Chronic ethanol increases systemic TLR3 agonist-induced neuroinflammation and neurodegeneration. *Journal of Neuroinflammation* 2012, **9**:30.

"**Background**: Increasing evidence links systemic inflammation to neuroinflammation and neurodegeneration. We previously found that systemic endotoxin, a TLR4 agonist or TNFalpha, increased blood TNFalpha that entered the brain activating microglia and persistent neuroinflammation. Further, we found that models of ethanol binge drinking sensitized blood and brain proinflammatory responses. We hypothesized that blood cytokines contribute to the magnitude of neuroinflammation and that ethanol primes proinflammatory responses. Here, we investigate the effects of chronic ethanol on neuroinflammation and neurodegeneration triggered by toll-like receptor 3 (TLR3) agonist poly L:C."

"**Conclusions**: Chronic ethanol potentiates poly L:C blood and brain proinflammatory responses. Poly L:C neuroinflammation persists after systemic responses subside. Increases in blood TNFalpha, IL-1beta, IL-6, and MCP-1 parallel brain responses consistent with blood cytokines contributing to the magnitude of neuroinflammation. Ethanol potentiation of TLR3 agonist responses is consistent with priming microglia-monocytes and increased NOX, ROS, HMGB1-TLR3 and markers of neurodegeneration. These studies indicate that TLR3 agonists increase blood cytokines that contribute to neurodegeneration and that ethanol binge drinking potentiates these responses."

27. Allan Siegel, Suresh Bhatt, Rekha Bhat, and Steven S Zalcman, The Neurological Bases for Development of Pharmacological Treatments of Aggressive Disorders. *Current Neuropharmacology* 2007 June; 5 (2): 135-147.

"Violence and aggression are major causes of death and injury, thus constituting primary public health problems throughout much of the world costing billions of dollars to society. The present review relates our understanding of the neurobiology of aggression and rage to pharmacological treatment strategies that have been utilized and those which may be applied in the future. Knowledge of the neural mechanisms governing aggression and rage is derived from studies in cat and rodents. The primary brain structures involved in the expression of rage behavior include the hypothalamus and midbrain periaqueductal gray. Limbic structures, which include amygdala, hippocampal formation, septal area, prefrontal cortex and anterior cingulated gyrus serve important modulating functions. Excitatory neurotransmitters that potentiate rage behavior include excitatory amino acids, substance P, catecholamines, cholecystokinin, vasopressin, and serotonin that act through 5-HT2 receptors. Inhibitory neurotransmitters include GABA, enkephalins, and serotonin that act through 5-HT1 receptors. Recent studies have demonstrated that brain cytokines, including IL-1β and IL-2, powerfully modulate rage behavior. IL-1β exerts its actions by acting through 5-HT2 receptors, while IL-2 acts through GABAA or NK1 receptors. Pharmacological treatment strategies utilized for control of violent behavior have met with varying degrees of success. The most common approach has been to apply serotonergic compounds. Others included the application of antipsychotic, GABAergic (anti-epileptic) and dopaminergic drugs. Present and futures studies on the neurobiology of aggression may provide the basis for new and novel treatment strategies for the control of aggression and violence as well as the continuation of existing pharmacological approaches."

28. Rajeshwara N. Achur, Willard M. Freeman, Kent E. Vrana, Circulating Cytokines as Biomarkers of Alcohol Abuse and Alcoholism *Journal of Neuroimmune Pharmacology* March 2010, Volume 5, Issue 1, pp. 83-91.

"There are currently no consistent objective biochemical markers of alcohol abuse and alcoholism. Development of reliable diagnostic biomarkers that permit accurate assessment of alcohol intake and patterns of drinking is of prime importance to treatment and research fields. Diagnostic biomarker development in other diseases has demonstrated the utility of both open, systems biology, screening for biomarkers and more rational focused efforts on specific biomolecules or families of biomolecules. Long term alcohol consumption leads to altered inflammatory cell and adaptive immune responses with associated pathologies and increased incidence of infections. This has led researchers to focus attention on identifying cytokine biomarkers in models of alcohol abuse. Alcohol is known to alter cytokine levels in plasma and a variety of tissues including lung, liver, and very importantly brain. A number of cytokine biomarker candidates have been identified, including: TNFα, IL1α, IL1β, IL6, IL8, IL12, and MCP-1. This is an emerging and potentially exciting avenue of research in that circulating cytokines may contribute to diagnostic biomarker panels and a combination of multiple biomarkers may significantly increase the sensitivity and specificity of the biochemical tests aiding reliable and accurate detection of excessive alcohol intake."

29. Mommersteeg P.M., Vermetten E., Kavelaars A., Geuze E., Heijnen C. J., Hostility is related to clusters of T-cell cytokines and chemokines in healthy men. *Psychoneuroendocrinology* 2008 Sep; 33(8): 1041-50.
"Hostility was significantly related to decreased IL-6/chemokine secretion and increased pro- and anti-inflammatory cytokines. There was an inverse relation between age and hostility scores. Early life trauma and depression were positively and independently related to hostility as well. This study represents a novel way of investigating the relation between cytokines and psychological characteristics. Cytokines/chemokines clustered into functional factors, which were related to hostility in healthy males. Moreover this relation appeared to be independent of reported depression and early trauma."

30. Liya Qui, Jun He, Richard N. Hanes, Olivera Pluzarev, Jau-Shyong Hong and Fulton T. Crews, Increased systemic and brain cytokine production and neuroinflammation by endotoxin following ethanol treatment. *Journal of Neuroinflammation* 2008, **5**: 10.

"Results: LPS increased proinflammatory cytokines (TNFα, MPC-I, IL-1β) several fold in liver, brain and serum at 1 hr. Ethanol is known to increase liver cytokines and alter the risk of multiple chronic diseases. Ten daily doses of ethanol increased brain and liver TNFα, and pretreatment with ethanol potentiated LPS-induced increases in TNFα, MCP-I, IL-1β in liver, serum and brain. Proinflammatory cytokine levels in liver and serum returned to basal levels within a day, whereas brain proinflammatory cytokine remained elevated for long periods. IL-10, an anti-inflammatory cytokine, is reduced in brain by ethanol and LPS, while brain proinflammatory cytokines remain increased, whereas liver IL-10 is increased when proinflammatory cytokines have returned to control levels."

"Conclusion: Acute increases in serum cytokines induce long lasting increases in brain proinflammatory cytokines. Ten daily doses of ethanol exposure results in persistent alterations of cytokines and significantly increases the magnitude and duration of central and peripheral proinflammatory cytokines and microglial activation. Ethanol induced differential and anti-inflammatory cytokine Il-10 responses in liver and brain could cause long lasting disruption of cytokine cascades that could contribute to protection or increased risk of multiple chronic diseases."

31. Wolfgang J Streit, Robert E Mrak and W Sue T Griffin, Microglia and neuroinflammation: a pathological perspective. *Journal of Neuroinflammation* 2004, 1:14.

"This new understanding has come from rapid advances in the field of microglial and astrocytic neurobiology over the past fifteen to twenty years. These advances have led to the recognition that glia, particularly microglia, respond to tissue insult with a complex array of inflammatory cytokines and actions, and that these actions transcend the historical vision of phagocytosis and structural support that has long been enshrined in the term "reactive gliosis." Microglia are now recognized as the prime components of an intrinsic brain immune system, and as such they have become a main focus in cellular neuroimmunology and therefore in neuroinflammation. This is not the inflammation of the adaptive mammalian immune response, with its array of specialized T-cells and the made-to-order antibodies produced through complex gene rearrangements. This is, instead, the innate immune system, upon which adaptive immunity is built."

32. David M. Buss, *The Dangerous Passion: Why Jealousy Is As Necessary As Love and Sex* (New York: The Free Press, A Division of Simon & Schuster, Inc., 2000) p. 83.

"A number of possible explanations exist for the modest link between alcohol consumption and jealousy. First, alcohol may lower a man's inhibitions, causing him to vent suspicions that he already has. Second, men who are concerned about their troubled marriages may be more prone to drink heavily, thus creating a link between alcohol and jealousy. Third, alcohol may directly affect jealousy, creating suspicions that were not previously present by distorting perceptions, producing errors in logic, or twisting the interpretation of facts."

33. lvdailytimes.com, April 18, 2013 11:25 A.M. posting of New Mexico State Police report.

34. City of Las Vegas (New Mexico) Media Release, November 5, 2012, RE: Uniform Crime Reporting Statistics.

35. Reese Witherspoon and her husband were released from jail in Atlanta, Friday morning, April 19, 2013. Her statement was issued the following Sunday and appeared in USA Today. The videos of her intoxicated conversation are from Hollywood.com.

36. James Graham, *The Secret History of Alcoholism: The Story of Famous Alcoholics and Their Destructive Behavior* (Rockport, MA: Element Books, 1996).

37. Gibson's Anti-Semitic Tirade—Alleged Cover Up, tmz.com, 7/28/2006.

38. *Singer Says Arrest "Valuable Lesson"* Albuquerque Journal A, 4 Wednesday, November 26, 2003. *Campbell Blames Anxiety Drug*, the Associated Press, via the Albuquerque Journal, D, 1 Thursday, November 27, 2003.

39. *The country star who became the voice of heartbreak.* The Week May 10, 2013.

40. *Physically Abused Children Recognize the Face of Anger*, Erica Goode, The New York Times, June 18, 2002.

This article references a study appearing in *The Proceedings of the National Academy of Sciences*, which demonstrated that abused children are quicker to recognize facial changes toward anger. It is part of their adaptation process—they are more aware faster than children who haven't been abused.

41. *Skater Harding Arrested on Violence Charge.* Yahoo! News February 23, 2000.

42. *Jamie Lee Curtis.* Entertainment Tonight September 27, 2000.

43. *Man Allegedly Drank 8 Shots,* Guillermo Contreras, Albuquerque Journal, October 6, 2000, D, 2.

44. *N. Y. Woman May Leave Jail Today,* Guillermo Contreras, Albuquerque Journal, March 23, 2000, D, 1.

45. *Lawyer Fined Over Air Rage Bourbon Binge,* Travel Voice, June 3, 2000.

46. *Brouhaha Lands Jet At Sunport* Police remove 16 passengers after ruckus reported over free-drink coupons, alcohol service, Jeff Jones, Albuquerque Journal, December 1, 2000, A, 1.

47. *Briton Extradited over Air Rage Attack,* ananova.com, November 9, 2000.

48. *Bangor Is U.S. Hub for Air Rage Arrests,* APBnews.com June 13, 1999.

49. *Increase in air-rage reports may force alcohol limits,* Naedine Joy Hazell, The Hartford Courant via The Albuquerque Journal September 9, 2001 E, 1.

50. *Alcohol Ban on Flights Possible,* Moscow, Albuquerque Journal, February 16, 2007 A, 9.

51. *Angry passengers complained after a boozed-up off-duty British Airways crew ran amok during a flight.* thesun.co.uk, March 2, 2013.

52. *Unruly Passenger Kicked Off Hong Kong Flight,* Reuters, January 9, 2001.

53. *Woman's In-flight Antics Land Her in Anchorage Jail after Jet Diverted,* Casey Grove, Anchorage Daily News, August 20, 2013.

54. *Woman Accused of Pepper-spraying,* the Santa Fe New Mexican via the Albuquerque Journal, February 17, 2013, B, 6.

55. *Men Who Slashed Faces Of Bartenders Get 1 Year,* S. U. Mahesh, Journal Northern Bureau, Albuquerque Journal, December 16, 1998, D, 8.

56. *Smith Charged In Fight,* Dave Saltonstall, New York Daily News via Albuquerque Journal, October 24, 1993, A, 1.

57. *Britain: a nation 'in grip of drink crisis',* Martin Bright and Gaby Hinsliff, The Guardian, Sunday, November 21, 2004.

58. *Abuse Accusations Plague Key West Police Department*, Nick Madigan, The New York Times, May 4, 2003.

59. *Drunken Mob Kills Out-of-Tune Singer*, Albuquerque Journal, July 7, 1998, C, 4.

60. H. Joe Wang, Samir Zakhari, M. Katherine Jung, Alcohol, inflammation, and gut-liver-brain interactions in tissue damage and disease development, *World Journal of Gastroenterology*, 2010 March 21; 16(11): 1204-1313.

61. *The Neuroimmunological Basis of Behavior and Mental Disorders*, Allan Siegal and Steven S. Zalcman, editors (New York: Springer, 2009).

Note the chapter entitled Cytokines and Aggressive Behavior by Alan Siegal, Suresh Bhatt, Rekha Bhatt, and Steven S. Zalcman. The following appears on page 235 at the beginning of the chapter:

"Abstract. Studies conducted in rodents, primates and humans have provided evidence that proinflammatory cytokines may play an important [role] in the regulation of aggression and rage behavior. More recent studies conducted in the cat have generated more direct evidence of cytokine involvement in modulating rage behavior. Activation of IL-1 receptors in the medial hypothalamus and periaqueductal gray (PAG) potentiates defensive rage behavior in the cat. Facilitation of defensive rage is mediated trough 5-HT2 receptors in the medial hypothalamus and PAG. Activation of IL-2 receptors in the medial hypothalamus and PAG differentially affect defensive rage behavior. In the medial hypothalamus, IL-2 receptors suppress defensive rage and this effect is mediated through

GABAA receptors; in the PAG, IL-2 receptors facilitate the occurrence of defensive rage behavior and such effects are mediated through substance P NK1 receptors. With respect to peripheral mechanisms, LPS administration induces the release of a cascade of proinflammatory cytokines. Among the cytokines released, TNFα appears to play a significant role in the induction of the suppressive effects of LPS upon defensive rage and in sickness behavior in the cat. Concerning the central mechanisms regulating LPS induced suppression of defensive rage and sickness behavior serotonin 5-HT1A and PGE2 receptors in the medial hypothalamus appears [sic] to play key roles in controlling these processes."

"Introduction. Interest in the possible role of cytokines in emotional behavior in general and in aggressive behavior in particular is derived from evidence in the literature suggesting a reciprocal relationship between immune function and aggressive behavior."

Made in the USA
Columbia, SC
22 October 2017